WRITE NOW

Write A Book Even If You Have Never
Written Before

RAAM ANAND

STARDOM BOOKS
WORLDWIDE
www.StardomBooks.com

STARDOM BOOKS
A Division of Stardom Publishing
and infoYOGIS Technologies.
105-501 Silverside Road
Wilmington, DE 19809

SECOND EDITION JANUARY 2022

Stardom Books

WRITE NOW

Write A Book Even If You Have Never
Written Before

Raam Anand

p. 184
cm. 13.5 X 21.5

Category: Self-help/Writing/
Business/Marketing/Influence/Persuasion

ISBN-13: 978-1-7369486-9-9

DEDICATION

This book is dedicated to all my gurus, mentors, and great advisors. I stand on the shoulders of those giants who came before me. All those amazing souls who had the guts and perseverance to overcome the insurmountable challenges that life threw at them and thrived successfully to tell their stories of struggles, successes, and triumphs. The content in this book is a small reflection of the incredible teachings and thought-provoking philosophies of my great gurus.

CONTENTS

ACKNOWLEDGMENTS

You have seen this often. You pick up a book and get to this section, and find that the author, once again, has dedicated the book to someone else and not to you. Some unknown, non-existent assistant or some casual reference to famous people.

Not this time.

I would like to thank YOU for taking the time to get this book. I would be even more grateful if you read the book and take ACTION to further your life and create a positive difference. I would consider this book a success if it inspires you enough to become an internationally published, bestselling author.

ACTION GUIDES
for all these amazing books

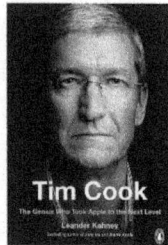

Includes **Book Summary, Reading Plan, Capture Ideas and Action Plan** for each book.

Register your copy of this book and
Download all the action guides for free:
http://RaamAnand.com/action-guides/

1

WHY SHOULD I WRITE
A BOOK NOW?

BIG IDEA: If you want to do anything with anyone, first you need to get their attention and trust, the two most critical elements of communication. A book helps you get both by sharing your valuable message in the pages of your book.

The world is in chaos. If there is anything people need right now, it is hope and help. When you publish your non-fiction story and share what you have been through, your struggles, what you have learned, or what you have overcome, you become the voice of hope and help.

People do not need ground-breaking new inventions or out-of-this-world techniques in a book. All they need is perspective, some insights, and a direction to follow. If people need information, they Google it. If they need perspective, wisdom, direction, or coaching, they need you. They need someone who has a little bit more knowledge than themselves.

They need someone who has seen it, done it, or experienced it (the topic) so that they can guide them in the right direction. If you are someone who has had the idea of authoring a book but has not taken to it yet, then my friend, this is the best time for you to realize that dream. Although many people know that writing a book will change the trajectory of their life, they just don't do it as they are not familiar with the process. Just like anybody can dance, anybody can write a book, with enough preparation and guidance. You will be scared until you dip your feet into the water. Once you get comfortable, no one can stop you from swimming your way to the other side.

Now, Let's Take a Deeper Look into Why You Should Write a Book.

1. Send Out A Message:

Let's say you are writing a book about the hurdles people face in their lives and the different ways to overcome them. A book on this topic is very necessary to the youngsters of today, considering the times we live in. Your aim is to tell people not to lose hope and to hang in there. Writing a book will help you get your suggestions out in the world.

Plus, you will cherish this piece of writing your entire life. People will look up to you for the important lessons shared in your book. So, whatever may be the subject, do not hesitate to talk about it. You never know; your book might end up being a guide to thousands or even millions of people!

2. A Book Raises Your Visibility And Gets Media Coverage:

When a media outlet wants a comment on something, whose opinion do they solicit? Obviously, they ask the experts.

And how do they know if someone is an expert? They recognize experts by the books they have authored.

You might have noticed some people in your field getting a lot more attention than you, just because they are published authors. Even if your knowledge stacks up better when compared to theirs, they will be chosen over you because they have the added title of being 'a bestselling author' to their identity. Therefore, if you want visibility in your field and seek media coverage, being an authority and an expert is vital, and one of the best ways of being an authority is to author a book about your topic. Once you have a book under your belt, getting media coverage becomes ten times easier. And, this is not the case just for the media.

The program managers of some of the most prestigious arenas you would love to enter, like lecture halls, television studios, boardrooms, social media pages, etc., regularly seek and solicit authors as speakers. Becoming a published author opens up a number of incredible opportunities in the long run.

3. Put Yourself On The Map:

When you publish a book, you get enlisted on the Internet as the author of that book. Let us say you have written a book on the topic of losing weight by choosing a proper diet. Consider this scenario: Sharon, a young lady, is looking to lose weight. She is seeking information on the Internet on different dietary habits and various workouts.

Now, there are thousands of people claiming to be weight-loss instructors on the Internet. Sharon is confused and does not know whom to trust or which weight-loss regime to choose, as there are many seemingly good options. While she is on this quest, she comes across your book on weight loss. The fact that you have written a whole book on weight loss makes her believe that you are a credible source, which you are, of course.

Hence, Sharon will most likely choose you over all the other weight-loss instructors on the Internet. In fact, she will come back for more of your content; she might even recommend you to her friends. This way, your book has the ability to make you even more popular and well-known.

When people look for help in their decision-making process to buy a product, they turn to the experts or authorities. Just like the media, they look for the person who literally "wrote the book" on the topic. Having a good book brings people to you; it lets people know who you are, and it shows them how you can help them (*"Entrepreneur Magazine"*). It is the best marketing tool you could ever use, not just to build your brand but to actually attract clients and influence people in a positive way at an incredibly low cost.

4. Increase Your Credibility:

The more well-known you become as an author, the more credible you are perceived. For instance, a person new in town has come down with a fever and is looking for good doctors to consult. He goes on the Internet and comes across a thousand doctors.

Now, how will he choose the best one? A quick search on Google shows an interesting book on the topic, authored by you, the Doctor. This book is a stamp for your credibility. This way, you have a clear advantage over the other experts. Therefore, a book can also double-up as a powerful promotional tool.

5. Leave A Good First Impression:

Let me ask you a question. You are in a business meeting, and your partner introduces you to one of his clients as a published author. What do you think the opposite person's impression will be of you? They will look at you as an expert because writing a book calls for a lot of experience and expertise. The person will believe that you are good at what you do and even recommend you to his colleagues. Think of all the doors of opportunity that are going to open because of your book!

6. You Will Be Contributing To A Better Tomorrow:

Let us say money-making is not your intention. Well, that is no problem. Writing a book is not just about making money. People write non-fiction books to make themselves familiar to the world and spread their message across.

Money is just a by-product. By writing a book, you are guiding other people who are as passionate as you are to follow a certain path or direction. It is our responsibility to pass on the knowledge, experience, expertise, and insights to the next generation. A book is a great tool for the furtherance of such ideas for the good of the community, the country, and the world at large.

7. Capture People's Attention:

Attention is one of the two most important things that everyone needs. The other is trust. We covered this earlier in this chapter. Let us say you are in charge of selling the products or services of your company. How would you do it? The first step would be to attract people's attention, right? Once you have their attention, you demonstrate how your product or service benefits them, and then they buy it.

Let us say your firm is hiring and you want to attract the best candidates. How can you do this? You will have to capture the attention of the potential candidates and show them why they should join your company. Again, we notice that the first step is getting attention.

Want to raise money? Grab the attention of VCs, angel investors, and PE funds with a spectacular pitch. Want to be invited to talks and events? Put yourself on the map; tell people about who you are and what you do. Promote yourself on all social media platforms. You get the drift, right? Now, how to get this valuable attention? There are many ways, but in my experience, writing and publishing a book is not only one of the best ways to get attention, but it is also one of the most underutilized strategies adopted by people. It is powerful, it is magical, and you can do it too.

8. How Does A Book Get You Attention?

Publishing a book is one of the best ways of getting attention and gaining trust; it is a multipurpose marketing tool. Your book can help you with almost anything you want: sales, media publicity, word-of-mouth publicity, recognition as an authority, etc. Below are a few more advantages of writing a book.

9. Authority, Credibility, And Expertise:

It is a widespread opinion that "a book is the new business card." However, I am of the dissenting opinion because just about anyone can have a business card. You could go to a print shop and get business cards, but you cannot just author a book at a print shop. What I like to say instead is that "your own book is the new college degree."

Four decades ago, only about 10 percent of people could go to college. A college degree was an indication of credibility and authority. But, the 'college' is not an exclusive domain anymore; it does not carry the same gravitas it once did. So, what can be considered as a sign of credibility and authority today, while also remaining authentic and rare?

Getting your book published, of course!

Writing a book shows that you have the courage to put your thoughts out there and you can commit and follow through. It shows you are the type to get things done, things that are hard and prestigious, and that involve a great deal of effort and persistence. Most people do not have it within themselves to take that risk: to set themselves up to be judged, and to show the world what they stand for.

10. A Book Helps People Talk About You

There is no better marketing than word-of-mouth. When someone whose opinion you trust tells you to do something, you generally listen and follow their advice. The best marketing tool you could hope for is to have other people talk about you and your business.

Nothing enables word-of-mouth better than a book you have authored. Your book puts your story in your words into other people's mouths.

So, when they talk about you, they are just saying what you want them to say! A good book causes people to repeat your terms, phrases, and ideas to other people. Imagine someone at a cocktail party who has read your book, talking to someone else in your potential audience. What would they say? Imagine what you want them to tell the other person. Picture that conversation occurring as a natural happenstance between two people. You can almost construct the positioning and narrative of your book from that conversation. If you can write a book that is valuable to people, they will WANT to talk about your book to others who have the problem you are trying to address.

Why? Because that makes THEM look better. That is how word-of-mouth works.

QUICK ASSIGNMENT:

Complete these sentences.

1. I   wish   to   write   a   book   because
   _____

   (Why do you wish to write a book?)
2. I   could   write   a   book   on
   _____

   (Topic you want to write about.)
3. The group of people I want to reach include
   _____

   (Your target audience or readers.)

RESOURCE: VIDEO

Visit: https://stardompublishing.com/evenmoreinfo/
-or-
Scan this to play the video

2

HOW DO I GET STARTED
WITH THE BOOK?

BIG IDEA: The most difficult part of becoming an author is getting started. The decision to become an author requires a little nudge and some courage. Once started, the project snowballs itself into an incredible asset for you.

Deciding to write a book is a huge deal. So, congratulations on beginning your journey. In the first chapter, we learned why you should write a book. In this chapter, I will help you get started with the process.

When first-time authors think about a book, the first question that comes to their mind is, "What topic should I write about?". Often, first-time authors fail because they start their book by choosing a topic and just getting on with writing.

It is like trying to construct a building without a plan or a foundation. With this beginning, the project is bound to fail.

This is exactly why many aspiring authors find themselves facing 'writer's block', the state where the flow of ideas comes to a grinding halt and nothing more can be written. The 'blank page' effect sets in. So, what can one do instead?

Start with your aspirations. What is 'that next big leap' that you are planning to achieve in your life, career, business, or profession? What do you want to achieve at this stage? What are your specific goals for the future? For some people, it is lead generation. For some others, it is publicity. For someone else, it could be media exposure or thought leadership, or the idea of leaving a legacy behind. Every successful author has one or two primary goals attached to their book. In fact, when aspiring authors start working with our publishing advisors at Stardom Books, this is the first exercise we walk them through.

The advisor asks a bunch of questions that help the author gain one hundred percent clarity on the reason, goal, and purpose of their book project. Once that is done, choose your target audience. Here is an example: One of our clients, Dr. Narayan Hulse, wrote a book on joint replacement surgeries. Now, joint problems are not very common in youngsters; however, a few people in their thirties might have undergone joint replacement surgeries. Who do you think the target audience here is? It is obviously the elderly people. The takeaway from this example is: Your book may or may not apply to everyone. Since you cannot cater to everyone's needs, it is essential that you pick a target audience and cater to their needs exclusively. In this book on joint replacement surgeries, although there might be a chapter or two on younger patients, the target audience is mainly those above the age of 45.

There is no fun in first writing your book and THEN looking for readers. It is always better to find the readers, analyze their needs, wants, and requirements, and then write a book based on what THEY want to know on your topic. Does it make sense? If you are on social media, then that is great. If you are not, get acquainted with it. Social media can help you research and understand your target audience. Let us say you are writing a self-help book.

Check out the most read 'self-help' related articles. Check out the most liked 'self-help' related posts. Doing this will help you structure your book better.

Here Are Some Pointers That Can Help You Understand Your Target Audience:

1. Make a note of the age group your readers belong to.
2. Where are they located?
3. What questions are they asking?
4. What is their financial status?
5. What problems are they facing related to your topic?
6. How can your book help them?
7. What other books are available to them?
8. What has not already been said?
9. What would be a watershed message in this area?
10. How can you get their attention?

Remember, you have not chosen your topic yet at this stage. Asking and answering these questions will reveal the most important problems, questions, and conversations that are happening with your target audience. Once this is done, you will have enough data points to suggest specific topics to solve specific problems. Non-fiction books should solve problems, provide solutions, or inform or educate the readers.

At Stardom Books, our authors find this exercise extremely interesting and thought provoking. They will be able to find the right alignment with their goals and their readers' goals with specific topic ideas. Usually, they end up with not just one but five to six book ideas at this stage.

You can then choose the topic that best resonates with you as your first book project. Who says you have to write just one book?

Once you have a topic, get cracking on the outline of your book. If you start your book without an outline, you are just navigating without a map.

The answers to the questions above are basically the content of your outline. All you now need to do is add some structure and organize the ideas into separate categories. The job here is to place all the information you have under various sections and chapters. The outline will be the foundation of your book. The next step is to write every day. No matter how busy you are, make sure to keep aside an hour or two every day for your book project, if you are doing it on your own.

At Stardom Books, first-time authors work with our trained publishing advisors who also doubles up as their accountability partners. Together, they develop the manuscript. This way, we ensure that the author's goals are in focus all the time and the readers' expectations are also met.

If you can work with a publishing advisor or a mentor, the project becomes much easier and the entire process will be fun and fulfilling. If you are on your own, you will have to motivate yourself and seek professional help whenever required.

Now, unlike fiction, the authors must state facts and give references while writing a non-fiction book. So, it is important to research your topic and get your facts right. Do not write what you want to say. Write what the readers want to know. You might want to present many things and showcase your expertise; while that is not wrong, if it is your first book, write about what the readers must know and something that will help the readers in their personal or professional areas. Imagine people referring to your book and making a key decision.

Book writing is an art that you learn. It is normal to feel out of place and nervous during the manuscript creation stage. It is bound to feel like a difficult task initially, so make sure not to give up. Just keep the end result in mind and work toward it.

If you ever get stuck, ask yourself this: Why am I writing this book? What's the point of writing this book? What will my life be like once this book is out? Find answers to these questions, and you will be on the right path once again.

By Deciding To Write a Book, You Will...
1. Take a deeper look at your own self. Writing a book is a self-exploration journey.
2. Have a professional piece of work under your belt. This will help you attract clients.
3. Help people find their passion, purpose, or meaning.
4. Attract better career opportunities.
5. Have something to cherish throughout your life.

Here Are the Biggest Needle Movers:
1. Identify your aspirations/goals.
2. Research the group of people you want to reach.
3. Decide your book topic and create the outline.

RESOURCE: VIDEO

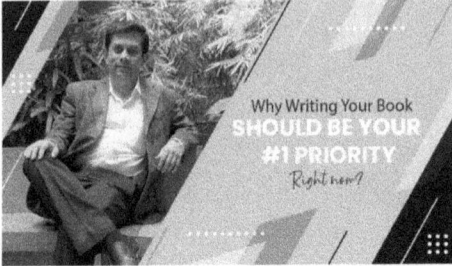

Visit: https://stardompublishing.com/evenmoreinfo/
-or-
Scan this to play the video

3

HOW DOES A BOOK TURN ATTENTION INTO MONEY?

BIG IDEA: Your own book is not just a bunch of printed sheets of pulp. It is a business or a professional asset that can produce terrific long-term results as well.

Attention is great, but most people do not just want to stop at that. When a book can fetch you popularity along with a few bucks, then why not? As I mentioned in the first chapter, a book is a versatile marketing tool that will draw attention, which can be turned into almost anything else you want. Let us make this concept even simpler:

Book = Attention = Money

1. A Book Can Launch A Consulting And Coaching Business:

Every consultant will hit a wall at some point in his/her career. Despite their successes till that point, they find it hard to pick themselves up. This is where a book can help you scale, not only that wall, but even greater heights. There are many instances where a book has taken consultants and coaches, including trainers, from being a small-time business or just a side hustle with a few clients to building an actual business with a large client base. It is at this point you might have a question.

"If I were to write a book talking about what I know, why would people want to hire me as a consultant when they could simply read what I have written?" Well, the book is HOW people find you. Companies and people hire consultants and coaches to teach them and their teams how best to implement their ideas; they do not bring them in to rehash the knowledge in their book.

The book is how you show them why you are worth hiring. Your book will be a tool to find and educate your prospects even before they meet you. And an educated prospect is 100 times more likely to hire you because you have already earned their trust with your valuable information. In fact, this book is an educational tool for aspiring authors who are not professional writers.

It provides them with insights, ideas, and perspectives on becoming an author. Most people who read this book sign up for some of our book publishing programs, especially if they are keen to expand their influence or grow their business or profession. If you do not believe that statement, look no further than Amy Cuddy. In just a handful of years, she went from being an out-of-work researcher to a well-respected marketing and branding consultant. Today, her standing is so high that she is someone who can speak to groups such as the World Bank and the IMF. How did she reach such heights? Hard work is a given, but when asked, she credits it to the successes of her two books and how they put her on the map.

2. A Book Can Promote Another Product:

One of the most profitable ways to monetize a book is by using it to promote another product. If you were to search on Amazon for books with the terms 'lose weight' or 'eat paleo', you would see thousands of books, and a lot of them are essentially buyer's guides for food companies, supplements, and even one-off products.

Take Mark Sisson, for example. He is the one who started Primal Blueprint, and he has published nearly a dozen books about his version of the paleo diet. They are, without a doubt, great books. He not only sells them on Amazon, he even gives many of them away for free on his website.

These books promote the right eating habits and inform the readers about Mark's complete line of Primal Blueprint supplements and food that they can buy. Although the books do not overtly ask people to buy these products, they buy them anyway, thanks to the ease of access. His books, and the seemingly complementary products, dovetail perfectly.

Think about it: Would you otherwise respond to an advertisement about supplements? You probably would not. But what if a book teaches you what supplements you should take, and when and why you should take them? If you trust the book, you would also likely trust the supplement recommendations.

Since Mark has excellent books (and an equally excellent website) where his advice on eating is trustworthy, automatically, his supplement recommendations also gain more credibility and perhaps even entice readers to buy his brand of supplements.

> **TIP:** Convert existing product brochures into a book. Add additional details, articles, pictures, illustrations, customer testimonials, etc., to turn an uninteresting 'sales' brochure into a good book. Our trained publishing advisors at Stardom Books are experts in this area and can help you create such a book rapidly and deploy it in your market segments effectively.

3. A Book Can Sell Software/SaaS Products:

A book is an excellent way for a company to sell software, especially SaaS software. The best example is HubSpot. If you are familiar with the concept called inbound marketing, this is the company that invented it. So how did they promote it? This might not surprise you anymore, but among other things, they brought out a book called *Inbound Marketing*.

The book does not even pitch HubSpot all that much. It essentially advertises inbound marketing, and you don't need a detective to guess what happened next. Readers realized that using HubSpot software was the easiest way to do inbound marketing. So, not only did the book provide real value to the readers, but it also converted many of them into customers. This is exactly how it works with the book you are reading right now as well.

> **TIP:** Create an 'instruction' book on how to use your software. Add value with best-uses, resource list, case studies, etc. You could also give away the instruction book. to prospective users.

Yes, many of our authors signed up with us to create and publish their books because they got clarity, value, and ideas from reading this book.

4. A Book Can Sell A Video Course:

A book can be one of the best ways for you to generate leads for your video course. It is a sure-fire money-making marketing tool. If your book is about a concept that assures a high return on investment (RoI) for the reader, you should also create new content as an advanced version of what you cover in your book.

This advanced version could be in the form of a video course, and then you could charge money for access to that video course. It may sound ludicrous, but people will be willing to pay $500 or more for a video course than pay more than $25 for a book that could cover the same material. It might not seem so, but it is a rational decision from the mindset of the companies as people tend to learn better from video and audio material than they do from books.

Whether it is rational or otherwise does not matter; what should matter to you, if you were to write a book and use it to sell similar material as a video course, is a guaranteed way to make money. A great example of this is Mike Hallowell. He published a book about how to drive sales for a company, and the book, while also being very good, ended up attracting a lot of traffic toward his advanced video course.

The book could become your 'front-end' product that is inexpensive for people to buy and an extremely low-risk offer to make. When they experience the value inside the book, you can tell them something like, "If you like this book, then you will absolutely LOVE the course we have created for an even deeper understanding…" Works like a charm, always.

5. A Book Can Recruit Talented Employees To Work For Your Company:

One of the best ways to entice entrepreneurs and C-level executives alike into working with you is through a book. You could lay your vision for your company out in a book, and it can be a clincher in convincing people to come and work for you.

One can often overlook this method, but it can be useful. Zappos is one of the best examples. Not only did Tony Hsieh write his book, but he also wrote a different book about the culture at Zappos.

He gave the latter away for free on his company's website as a way to get people to come work for his company. To this day, the book is used and considered as the best lead-generator for recruitment at Zappos. Other examples include Narayana Murthy, founder of Infosys, and Indra Nooyi, CEO of PepsiCo.

6. A Book Can Help Draw Clients To Your Agency:

If you specialize in selling B2B services, such as marketing or advertising or other similar services, do not discount how huge an asset a book will be in drawing and closing clients. Just ask Neil Patel. He started and ran Kissmetrics, a company with an almost exclusive clientele of big brands and companies.

Whenever he walks into a room to pitch a CMO, he also brings with him copies of his books to reinforce all the points he makes. It is ten times more effective than brochures or anything else he could produce. I mean, how about all the media work that Gary Vaynerchuk does? Is not most of it ultimately about getting clients for his large agency?

7. A Book Can Launch And Promote Paid Mastermind Groups:

There is a reason why masterminds get paid so handsomely and why they are in demand. Clients who read their books and are impressed with their knowledge want to share their know-how within their groups. A great example is Jay Fiset. He has a group called *Mastermind Millions* and a book called *Mastermind Mentors Manual*. In his book, he tells the story of how he built and runs his mastermind group. He also talks of how he became such a successful networker and tried to expand his connections.

The book ended up driving many sign-ups for his group, which is a paid community and meet-up group. Another great example is Joe Polish, the author of the book *Piranha Marketing*. After this book, he launched his mastermind group called, *The Genius Network*, with membership fees starting at $10,000 and going up all the way to $25,000 for special events.

8. A Book Can Launch Workshops And Group Teaching Programs:

If you are a consultant and a speaker, you will be familiar with the activity called group workshops. Essentially, businesses bring in consultants to train their employees over a day or over a course of several days. Consultants are expected to help the employees better their performances. But why do companies do this? Why do these companies not just ask their employees to read a couple of books and up their game? The reason is simple: not many people take the time to read a book in its entirety.

However, if the person who wrote the book were to come in and give a speech and answer questions for a day, there would be actual learning taking place. You would have heard of Nancy Duarte, the author of *Resonate*. She now conducts workshops on how to apply the learnings from her book, which routinely sells out. Her book and workshops reinforce each other as the book leads people to the workshop, and she sells copies of her book to the people who attend her workshop (*"Huffpost"*).

Another much bigger example of this idea is Stephen Covey's book, *The 7 Habits of Highly Effective People*, which became a huge 'expert-empire' by itself—led by the book and followed by courses and training programs, and even training other coaches to train participants. In fact, the book and the training program became the de-facto corporate training curriculum in tens of thousands of organizations around the world, pumping in millions of dollars in revenue, royalties, and sales for the Stephen Covey company. You could do the same.

9. A Book Can Help You Raise Money:

A lot of entrepreneurs write *Medium* posts to raise money. That is okay, but it can work on a different scale when you have a good book. Shane Mac used this strategy to fund his first start-up business. His book had a candid and engaging story about how he runs his company. He would send copies to VCs before pitches, and it also helped him in the talent recruitment for his new company, Assist.

One iconic example is the book, *The Promise of a Pencil*. Though this book was about a charity and not a start-up, the principle remains the same. Adam Braun was able to generate a ton of interest and raise a lot of money for his charity through the book.

The point is to use the book as the pitch deck in advance; it tells your story so well that you would get VCs lining up asking if they could invest their money in you. Imagine you are

the VC for a moment. Who would you invest your money in? Someone who has started a business with a business card or an expert who wrote a book on the business, seeking investment to grow it? The choice is pretty obvious, isn't it?

10. A Book Can Get You Speaking Appearances:

One of the significant ways to get attention (and even make money) from a book is to use it to become a public speaker. A book is a calling card for a speaker and a necessity. A book is a way for people to know for sure that you are qualified to address their group on your topic even if they know nothing else. Kevin Kruse is one of the best examples in this case.

If you read his blog, *Author Journey to $100k*, you will learn how he made money in his first year as an author and speaker—he reached $70K in book sales and made a further $170K from his speaking gigs. On a personal note, in the year 2017, I conducted two international seminars in India. How did I find speakers to invite from different countries?

I looked for authors who had written books on the topic I was interested in and voilà, I had my panel. I was able to bring Sharon Lechter, co-author of the *Rich Dad Poor Dad* series of books, to speak with me on the stage and we did several events together.

Books, as a marketing avenue for conferences, are largely underexploited. We have been active participants in a conference called the *Genius Summit*. This conference is about vision technology, and it looks to pair venture capitalists with the inventors and thought leaders of that space. They record the entire conference and then turn it into a book, with which the conference host does two things:

- He sends copies of the book to his LPs or potential entrepreneurs, and he gets all the benefits of publishing a book without having to write it.
- He includes a copy of the book when he mails out the applications for each year's conference. It has tripled his re-up rate.

By spending $5 to mail a lovely book to past participants, he gets them to spend $500+ on a conference that is more than six months away. I have to say, it is a sweet deal, and not to mention, TED does this too. They even have their publishing imprint.

Hey! It's Time for Some Reflection:

1. Reflect on this fundamental question: How can you turn attention into money? Ponder over the various ideas mentioned in this chapter and decide what suits you best.
2. Try to come up with different strategies that can help you benefit financially from your book.
3. It is possible to think of different books for different purposes or outcomes.

4

WHO SHOULD WRITE A BOOK?

BIG IDEA: Finding and sharing your message to the world.

This is a commonly asked question. The answer is quite straightforward too. Anyone who has a message to share with the world should write a book. The next obvious question that follows is, "Am I eligible to write a book?" Well, the right questions to ask are the following: What is my message to the world? What do I stand for? What can I teach others?... You get the drift, right?

Creating a non-fiction book does not require a degree or even professional writing skills. All it needs is a good message or teaching points. The rest of the factors like writing skills, grammar skills, editing skills, and even marketing and distribution abilities can be outsourced nowadays. Another angle to explore is to understand how to use a book as a business tool to further your business, career, or profession. Let us see some examples.

1. Get Recognized As An Authority, A Thought Leader, Or An Influencer In A Field:

Often categorized as experts or specialists, these people write a book to create that value distinction as an author, thereby gaining instant recognition, a favorable reputation, and credibility with their audience. A good example is one of our authors, Subramanya, a certified financial planner. After he wrote his book *Awaken The Millionaire Within*, his reach increased, and his business doubled!

2. Generate Leads For A Business Or Service:

Businesses cannot thrive without leads because leads eventually become paying customers. A book can become a great source to generate leads for a business: Dr. Andrew Caster's book on LASIK surgery, for instance. I have discussed a personal story on how Dr. Caster's book changed my life in chapter 23.

If you have a product or a service, a 'lead-generation' book could open up a flood of new customers to your business or profession, who are pre-qualified and ready to buy. That is why finding and choosing the right goals for a book is the first step in our publishing programs at Stardom Books.

3. Share An Important Idea That Helps People:

Good ideas create movements when they are shared with the world. If you are someone who has an idea that can make the world a better place, you must write a book. When readers like your idea, they talk about it and recommend your book to other people. Most top-selling books become bestsellers not because of the distribution strategy or the marketing power of the author or publisher, but through word-of-mouth.

Books have the power to create massive movements and fuel revolutions around the world. When you write about your struggles, stories, and challenges, it creates a supporting environment for other people who are facing similar challenges and provides them hope and help. That is the basic ingredient for creating your own movement, is it not?

4. Launch Or Advance A Career:

No other marketing strategy is as good or works as efficiently as publishing a book to launch or advance a career. It is the only marketing strategy that pays back the author in terms of royalties from the sale of books, and at the same time, launches or advances a career. In fact, many entrepreneurs who have created their books with us at Stardom Books were previously employed at different organizations. When they reached a certain stage and wanted to start their own ventures and become entrepreneurs, they wrote a book on their topic as a launch-pad strategy. This helped them establish themselves as experts and launch a new career or advance an existing career to higher levels of productivity and effectiveness.

5. Leave A Legacy Behind:

Some authors also say, "I don't care about goals... I just want to write a book for myself or my family." This is a valid argument. People inevitably undergo struggles, and some want to document their journey and the lessons learned in a book. They want their readers to discover the nuggets of wisdom they have unearthed during their journey. There could not be a more reasonable and noble goal to write a book. We, at Stardom Books, have worked with a billionaire who documented his journey in the form of a book for this very reason. Some senior experts also write a 'memoir' of their life story, with a number of personal stories, life lessons, anecdotes, and opinions.

Points to Consider:

Re-evaluate and answer the questions you had previously considered:

- What is my message to the world?
- What do I stand for?
- Why is it important?
- How can I use a book to spread my message to the world?

RESOURCE: VIDEO

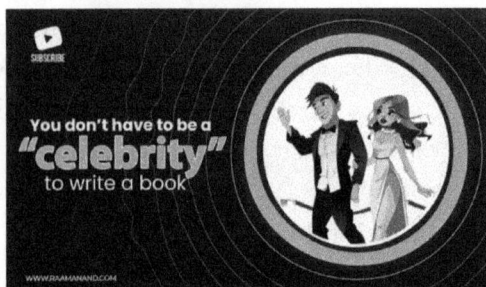

Visit: https://stardompublishing.com/evenmoreinfo/ -or- Scan this to play the video

5

I AM NOT GOOD AT WRITING. I ALSO DO NOT SPEAK ENGLISH. CAN I STILL BECOME AN AUTHOR?

BIG IDEA: Many first-time authors hesitate to publish a book just because their written-English is not exceptional. Here's how you can solve this issue permanently.

The landscape of the book industry, especially the non-fiction business book sector, has drastically changed. It is a level playing field now because the various platforms, starting with Amazon, have successfully democratized the publishing industry. Do you think good writers are born with a pen in their hands or words flowing out of their mouths? No!

It is a skill they learn. Some have a natural flair for words, and therefore it is easy for them to write. Then there are those who are born in countries where English is their first language.

They would have learned English as part of their standard education. Moreover, do you think all the classics we have today are written by native English authors? No, of course not! Take *The Alchemist* by Paulo Coelho, for instance. Coelho is a Brazilian lyricist and novelist. His novel was originally written in Portuguese and later translated into English. Did his being a Brazilian and not knowing the English language matter in any way? His book *The Alchemist* is one of the most widely read books, especially by English-speaking people. In fact, *The Alchemist* has been translated into more than 60 different languages. The author himself probably does not speak more than two or three languages!

The best thing about books is that they do not have borders and barriers. Books can be translated into any language or dialect and have the ability to reach the remotest corners of the world today, thanks to technological advancements over the last few decades. As Stephen King once said, "Books are a uniquely portable magic." How true is that? A good book can carry you to a different world altogether!

The belief that you need to know English to write a bestselling book is nothing but a total myth. If you wish to write your book in English, professional translators, editors, and writers are just a click away. As a form of creative expression, you can use any language to express your ideas or message to the world. Then you can hire talent on the Internet to accomplish the task of writing or re-writing your content in any language, including English.

If only English writers were to write English books, think of all the good literature we would have missed out on. You must have heard of Milan Kundera. Did you know that Kundera's books were banned in his native country, France, but managed to win awards in other countries after they were translated into English? Vladimir Nabokov is another incredible Russian author. His book *Lolita* is being read by thousands of people even today. *Voices from Chernobyl: The Oral History of a Nuclear Disaster* was also originally published in Russian and later translated into English. Even the famous *The Little Prince* was originally written in French by Antoine de Saint-Exupéry and later translated into English.

One of the most famous books from India, *Arthashastra*, is a dissertation on Economics, written in Samskrutam (Sanskrit) by Kautilya, the teacher to the founder of the Mauryan empire. The Nobel Prize–winning book *Gitanjali* by Rabindranath Tagore was originally written in Bengali and later translated into English. There are tens of thousands of examples like this to prove that language is just a way of expression and you do not need to have mastery over any particular language to express your ideas in a book.

Different languages have different ways of depicting emotions. Something that sounds lovely in French might not portray the same emotion when translated into English. So, a non-English writer writing a book in English will have that edge of depicting the right emotions over native English writers.

Take Haruki Murakami, for instance. Murakami, in all his books, brings out the uniqueness between Japanese and Western cultures. And sometimes, there are instances where people, after reading your translated work, prefer to go back and read the original version. Interestingly, most of Sigmund Freud's books were written entirely in German and later translated into English. Remember, all a reader looks for is good content. So, the language does not really matter.

With that said, if you are someone who can write in English but wants to improve on his skills, here are a few tips.

1. Read English books. Make notes of interesting words and carefully observe the content flow.
2. Listen to talks in English. This helps with your pronunciation. Movies and TV shows with sub-titles are a fantastic resource. TED talks and other online content are excellent as well.
3. Try to converse in English. Watching movies with English subtitles will also help.
4. Take a spoken English class.
5. Read English newspapers, and I mean, really read them. Refer to a dictionary when you do not understand a word.
6. If someone corrects your English while you are conversing, do not misinterpret it and take it to heart. Instead, thank them and learn from your mistakes.
7. Hire a translator. You can write the content in your native language and convey all your emotions to the translator the way they are meant to be. The translator can translate it, and the editor can then edit it. This is a much easier process.

Once, a young boy and his father were walking along a forest road. At some point, they stumbled upon a large tree branch on the ground. The boy asked his father, "If I try, do you think I could move that branch?" His father replied, "I am sure you can if you use all your strength."

The little boy tried his best to move the branch, but he was not strong enough, and he could not move it an inch from its place. He said with disappointment, "You were wrong, Dad. I cannot move it." "Try again," said his father. Again, the boy tried hard to push it. He struggled, but it did not move. "Dad, I cannot do it," said the boy.

Finally, his father said, "Son, I advised you to use all your strength. You did not. You did not ask for my help." We, at Stardom Books, are here to help you. It is okay if your language is not good. That is what our editors are there for. You just have to focus on spreading your message to the world and getting your basic or raw content on paper.

All that you need to publish a book today is to have a message to share. This message could be in any form, an idea or a set of points, or even a speech. Today, most non-writers can 'speak' their book using inexpensive technology and access to specialized manpower available at their fingertips.

In fact, some of our first-time authors have even 'spoken' their entire books, instead of actually writing them. They speak specific points into our mobile app which then gets automatically transcribed and sent to our editorial team for rewriting and polishing to go as content in the book. In terms of evolution, speech has undergone more significant development than writing. Humans started speaking hundreds of thousands of years ago while they only began writing on the walls of the caves about 10,000 years ago.

The form of writing we use today, in the way of books, started as recently as about 500 years ago, with the invention of the Gutenberg press, the first movable type printing press. Until then, all the wisdom was transferred from generation to generation via the oral medium.

Hundreds of thousands of experts are now able to disseminate their ideas throughout the world by combining technology with their authority on the subject matter in the form of books. Authors can now produce the audiobook first and then derive the text edition by transcribing the audio. It is reverse engineering in its simplest form. After an author has his idea or message transcribed, he will be able to find professional writers in any language, including English, to help him polish it.

Typically, the sweet spot for a non-fiction book is about 130-160 pages of content in a standard 8.5 inches by 5.5 inches book. In terms of word count, this is approximately 45,000 words of information. The average speed of everyday speech is about 130 words per minute. So, an excellent non-fiction book of about 45,000 words can be 'spoken' in just about 6 hours. It does not take years or months, or even weeks to create a book using this technique. Anyone who can speak about a topic with relevant information, irrespective of the language used, can produce a book in just hours.

Here is a Quick Diagram to Illustrate How This Works:

Brainstorm — Bunch of ideas or 'teaching' points — 1

Transform — Turn each point or idea into a question — 2

Record — Record answers to questions as audio — 4

Clarify — Answer each question in detail — 3

Draft — Transcribe the audio to get the first draft — 5

Refine — Get it professionally edited and proofread — 6

Publish — Make the book available for purchase — 7

So, essentially, authors in today's technology-driven world need not spend years in learning professional writing skills to become writers and publish a book. All you need is an idea or a message. Now that you have understood that language and writing skills cannot be given as excuses for not writing your own book, I would like you to list how many books you could publish on various topics!

RESOURCE: VIDEO

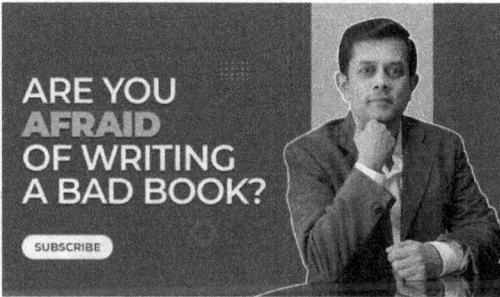

Visit: https://stardompublishing.com/evenmoreinfo/
-or-
Scan this to play the video

ARE YOU USING THE #1 STRATEGY FOR INFLUENCE, PR, BRANDING, SALES, MARKETING & CREDIBILITY?

SCHEDULE A FREE, NO-OBLIGATION APPOINTMENT WITH OUR PUBLISHING ADVISORS TO DISCUSS.

Schedule a free appointment with our Publishing Advisor to discuss your book idea:

http://StardomAlliance.com/meeting

6

I AM BUSY AND I DON'T HAVE TIME. HOW CAN I PUBLISH A BOOK?

BIG IDEA: This is another commonly asked question. If you are passionate about writing a book, not having enough time should not be an excuse. Give this chapter a read and ask yourself again if you really do not have the time to write.

"I have been too busy to write," "I have not had the time for it," "I am not in the mood to write," "I will start tomorrow," "I do not have my thoughts organized," "I am not experienced enough yet," "I do not have time to complete another online course," "I am already doing so much"… so on and so forth. We use statements like these to pacify ourselves and to reassure ourselves that we are doing fine, when in reality, we are not happy with where we are at. I have done this. You have done this. Everyone has done this to an extent. The excuses we give ourselves make us comfortable and somewhat content.

But those same excuses prevent us from meeting our goals, fulfilling our dreams, and helping the people we are meant to serve. These thoughts may reassure you for a moment, but it does not last. The next thing you know, you are settling in for the night, ready to catch up on the latest Netflix show you have been binge-watching, and you start to have thoughts like these: Maybe, I should get a job so that I am not so stressed about paying the bills. Would I still have some time to work on my business? How am I going to pay the bills this month if I do not find three new clients? Maybe this business is not right for me. I love my work, but I am never going to reach enough people to actually make this thing work, so I should probably give up.

The worst part of the whole situation is, in the back of your mind, you know you were meant to do bigger things and help people, but you are stuck. How long have you been thinking about writing a book? This probably is not a new idea for you, is it? And yet, how far have you gotten? If you are really honest with yourself, how much progress have you really made? Well, if you keep waiting for the right time, it will never come, and you will never write that book. There is never a perfect time. If you have to do it, you have to do it NOW.

A few months back, I had two calls with prospective authors, and, strangely, both were experts with similar business models. They both had valuable wisdom to share and could benefit greatly from writing a book. But, following our discussions, one of them decided that working with us did not make sense financially.

This person told me that he definitely wanted to do this someday and he would keep the idea in mind. However, he wanted to first increase the cash flow of his business, and said we could talk soon. It is now months later, and he is exactly where he was earlier—no increased influence and no closer to a book. He is just stuck in the same rut. The second person took a different track. He said that he was ready to get started even though he did not know where to begin, and was willing to spare some time for the project, a few hours per week, if not more. He asked what he could do that afternoon to start moving the book forward. I talked him through some roadblocks I anticipated he would run into, and he was on his way.

Now, a few months later, he is putting the finishing touches on his manuscript, and the book is set to be released next month. Do you see the difference between these two people? It has nothing to do with the value their book provides them, the quality of their idea, or even their work ethics.

The difference is that the second expert did not put off what was important to him. He found a way to get started immediately and dove in because he knew that *someday* is just a nicer way to say never.

If you are willing to learn how to work smarter and use your time wisely, you are a lot closer to reaching the next level than you think. Your path to success only remains elusive because you are still trying to find it using the old flashlight that has been in your junk drawer for years—the one you smack hard on the bottom a few times to make it work.

At Stardom Books, our coaching for book writing is the 10,000-watt stage light that illuminates your path to reaching thousands of people who need your help. It gives you the training, tools, and support you need to land and leverage publishing opportunities that catapult your business or career to the next level. There is a catch, though… I am going to ask you to do some scary things here. If you are scared of putting yourself out there, sharing your story, thoughts, and ideas in a way that gets them published, shared, and liked, and reaching out for support from your peers, then book writing is not the right project for you.

But one of the most amazing things about life is that you get to choose what you are scared of. Do not get disheartened if you feel intimidated, because you have our highly-trained publishing advisors and a close-knit group of fellow aspiring authors by your side. Let us address a major issue now. You have made up your mind to start writing, but you do not seem to find the time. I understand this can be exhausting. The good news is, I have got you covered. With the evolution of technology, in present times, this should not even be a worry. In fact, this is one of the reasons why I started my hybrid publishing house. If you look at our framework, I have explained in detail how you can 'speak' your book instead of 'writing' it.

Writing (or typing on a keyboard into a computer) slows down the flow of ideas from the mind, and even professional writers experience what is known as 'writer's block', a period of lull followed by a bout of writing. Writing, unless you are a professional writer, is not a very efficient way to create books. The better way is to 'speak' your book. However, answering the question at hand, if you are really passionate about authoring a book, being short on time should not bother you at all.

Despite all the distractions, you will somehow squeeze writing into your schedule. As discussed in the previous chapters, all it takes is about 5 hours of 'speaking' to create a book of about 40,000 words. You could easily complete an 80–120 page non-fiction book with that output.

We have developed these techniques for busy professionals who want to become published authors but are hard-pressed for time. The smartphone in our hands today is smart enough to record a speech that can then be transcribed by a professional somewhere across the world and then be modified and polished by another professional editor who could be in a different corner of the world.

If You Are Someone Who Likes to Write But Cannot Find The Time, Here Are Some Tips:

1. Start your day early and get some writing done before everyone else in the house wakes up. Writing for even 20 minutes a day makes a huge difference.
2. Nobody is born an author. Every perfect book has several rejected drafts. So do not worry about your language. Just get your thoughts on the paper.
3. Try to shut off the things that distract you. If it is your neighbour's dog, go to a nearby park or a nearby café/library and write. Find a suitable quiet place.
4. Just like how you never skip your meals, ensure that you keep to your commitment to writing. It should be a part of your everyday grind.
5. If you come across something that might help you with your book, make a note of it right there. Always carry a journal or use a journaling app on your mobile.
6. Some days might just be bad. You will be in no mood to write. However, do not let yourself off the hook with that excuse. However bad the day might be, get your daily dose of writing done. If you are not motivated enough, then ask a friend to help you. Our

publishing advisors often take the role of 'accountability partners' for aspiring authors.

7. To make the process of writing easier, create a book outline. Compose an introduction, be clear on what the chapters are and what will go into each of them, and work accordingly. Track the progress you have made every day. Having a deadline helps. As days pass by, you will notice that you are involuntarily writing every day.

8. Once you reach this stage, get your own writing space. Having a clean and tidy writing space will put you in a better mood. This can be an escape from your daily grind.

9. If you are happy with what you have written, treat yourself. This will keep you motivated. And, you are writing a book on something you love. So, it should not be a problem to come up with content. Whenever you find free time, just record whatever comes to your mind.

10. Use a text-to-speech converter app or have someone transcribe it for you. Use your commute time to research your content. Or make a note of it somewhere and get back to it as soon as possible. "Can I not wait and do this later, when things settles down?" Of course, you can, if you are okay with risking your idea being taken over by someone else.

To improve your thought flow, start reading other books. Look up a few books written on the topic you are exploring and read them carefully. Attend talks on the topic and make notes. Watch my "Online Book Publishing" videos (available at www.RaamAnand.com).

All we want you to do is take action and work on making your book a reality. Whether it is with us at Stardom Books (www.StardomBooks.com) or on your own—take action. There is STILL time to set aside everything else and join us to become a bestselling author. This is the best investment you will ever make for yourself.

Now that you have understood that being busy cannot be an excuse to not get started on your book, I want you to ponder on the following points:

1. Do you still think you do not have time to write?
2. The calendar is your best friend. Dedicate blocks of time on your calendar for the book project and you will be making great strides in no time at all!

"Take a good book to bed with you—books do not snore."
                                         – Thea Dorn

7

WHAT IS ISBN? WHY SHOULD I CARE ABOUT IT?

The International Standard Book Number (ISBN) is a numeric commercial book identifier. The publishing house usually buys this. These unique numbers are assigned to various book editions. Be it an e-book, a paperback, or a hardcover edition of the same book, all have different ISBNs. Although the author does not really have to worry about an ISBN, it does not hurt to learn a couple of things about it. ISBN is usually a 13-digit code for books that holds good internationally. This code captures information regarding the book's publisher, title, language, edition, and version. The method of assigning an ISBN is nation-specific and varies between countries, often depending on how large the publishing industry is within a country. Customers can identify and order the exact book they want to purchase using the ISBN. In fact, everyone depends on the ISBN to track purchases and sales—libraries, bookstores, online retailers, distributors, wholesalers, etc.

Let us Look at Some of The Common Questions Asked About ISBN:

1. **If I get an ISBN for my first book, can I re-use it for my next book?**

No. The code cannot be reused. It is one ISBN for each edition

2. **Can I not publish my book at all if I do not have an ISBN?**

Well, that is not true. If you are writing a book for your sake and just for a limited circle, which is not meant for commercial purposes, you do not need an ISBN.

3. **I am a self-publisher, and I do not want to invest in an ISBN. What are the disadvantages?**

Firstly, you will not be allowed to publish your book commercially if you do not have an ISBN. Even if you do, your book will not be available in physical bookstores. In other cases, even the online stores might not stock your books. ISBN helps you maximize your books' sales. It is also important if you want your book to be listed on Amazon, Flipkart, and other online portals. Most importantly, if you self-publish, even if you have an ISBN, your book will miss out on many major distributors who source books from publishers directly.

4. Tell me more about ISBN:

It is a 13-digit number, and it has five main parts:

- It is always prefixed by 978.
- The code contains a country identifier.
- The code helps identify your publisher.
- It also has your title and category identifier.
- Lastly, there is a check digit that validates the ISBN.

As mentioned earlier, the ISBN helps the book flow through the publishing industry and can be used to track sales and distribution. There are agencies in specific countries that issue ISBNs. All books published from a publishing house must carry an ISBN. To sweeten the pot, you should know that having an ISBN will get your book listed by Bowker's Books in Print, a database used by the major search engines, bookstores, and libraries worldwide. An ISBN also identifies the book's physical properties, such as trim size, page count, and binding type.

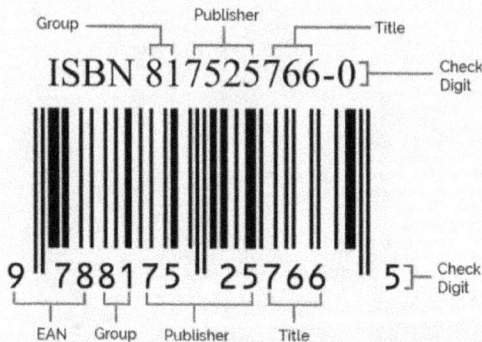

Books are good company, in sad times and happy times, for books are people – people who have managed to stay alive by hiding between the covers of a book.

- E.B. White

8

PUBLISHING STYLES

BIG IDEA: When you are writing a book, you should definitely consider the 'how' of publishing your book. If you have not thought about it yet, there is no need to fret. By the end of this chapter, you will have everything you need to know about the different publishing styles.

Unlike earlier days, the authors of today have several options to choose from.

Here Are Three Major Forms of Publishing:

- Traditional publishing.
- Self-publishing.
- Hybrid publishing.

1. Traditional Publishing

Here, you write a book and then hunt for an agent. The agent will in turn, pitch your book idea to publishers who are willing to consider it. You then sign a contract with them, and they publish the book on your behalf. The profits (royalties) are shared.

Pros:
- Publishing through recognized platforms helps you get instant fame. You get the support of agents. They help you navigate your career even after publishing your book, be it with book signing or book tours.
- Traditional publishers have in-house marketing, designing, editing, and proof-reading teams who constantly work to deliver the best outcome, greater reach, and increased popularity.
- Since an entire team of editors is at their service, the author can be at ease. The author can lay back and take his time with the book.
- Publishing via a traditional publishing house opens up many opportunities, like appearing on bestseller lists, being nominated for awards, and being reviewed in newspapers and other media.

Cons:
- Traditional publishers have lower royalty rates. Traditionally published authors receive anywhere from 7% to 15% royalties. Most often, they are not paid anything at all.

- There is no steady income of money for traditionally published authors. They receive royalty payouts twice a year.

- Once the team of editors at a traditional publishing house takes over, their editorial call will be considered final. The authors do not have a lot of say here about the title, book design, etc. The author cannot exercise creative content freedom here.

- Since the known traditional publishers usually have a list of books for publishing, your book might take a long time to get published. It may range from one year to four years.

- Here, the publisher is in demand. So, the author will have to make a lot of compromises. He/she may face many rejections and have to put up with the editors butchering the content. The publisher might not even issue a contract for the subsequent book if the first one does not sell well.

- By signing a book deal with a traditional publishing house, the author is basically giving up his/her rights to the content. This can get tricky at times.

2. Self-Publishing

A few authors like exercising full control over their content and the entire process of book publishing. They have to edit and format the book, design their book cover, do the marketing, buy the ISBN, and manage every little thing. Self-publishing calls for a lot of patience, mental peace, and energy. Self-publishing has indeed allowed a lot of authors to share their content, irrespective of the size of the book.

Pros:

- Authors who self-publish get 60% to 80% royalty rates. They receive monthly royalty payments.

- Here, the book creating process is faster. And, they do not have to bow to anyone. They reserve all the rights.

- Self-publishers have the opportunity to handpick their editors. They can get their books edited by professionals whom they trust. They can outsource the designing and formatting work to other people who are experts in the respective fields.

- Self-publishers do not have to worry about the publishing house editors not meeting the deadlines. Since it is their book, they can take as much time as they want and publish the book. Additionally, since they have all the freedom, they can publish whatever they want. The authors do not have to worry about editing guidelines or publishing house standards.

Cons:

- The marketing and promotion of the book can be one of the major disadvantages in self-publishing.

- Self-publishing is a good idea only if the author has good contacts and is already an established writer.

- Outsourcing editing work and hiring freelancers, and following up with them can get uncomfortable.

- Apart from paying for outside work, the self-publisher also has to take a lot of time away from her profession or work, which could become quite difficult over time and might defeat the purpose of writing the book in the first place.

- Without the right guidance, mentoring, and training, the project becomes extremely difficult to manage, and that is why many people who have self-published choose never to do so again.

There are many other cons of self-publishing. They are discussed in detail in the next chapter.

3. Hybrid Publishing

Hybrid publishing is what we do, at Stardom Books. Here the author is involved in the publishing process, and so is the publishing house. Our editors edit the content, and the sales team takes care of the marketing.

Hybrid publishing is the best of both worlds. It combines the best elements of traditional publishing and self-publishing.

Pros:

- Here, the author has his/her freedom. He is not dominated by the values of the publishing house, like in traditional publishing. The author and editors are on the same page, and both of them value each other's inputs. The authors have control over the content, and they are also involved in the entire process of publishing.
- The author has all the perks of self-publishing, but he/she will not have to worry about the marketing and other technicalities of publishing a book.
- Hybrid publishers are considerate and will value the authors' inputs. The authors are more like their partners. Authors are paid higher royalties, and more frequently, unlike in traditional publishing, where it is

paid only once or twice a year, depending on the profits.

- Hybrid publishers let the author be themselves. They make sure the author's voice is heard. The editing style is completely different from that of a traditional publishing house. The author's personality will reflect in the book.

Cons:

- Hybrid publishers cost you some initial project investment. The process is not free, like in self-publishing.
- Hybrid publishers do not have a huge name as a few traditional publishers do. This is one of the drawbacks. However, the cons do not outweigh the pros!
- Some people still consider being traditionally published as more prestigious, which is just a myth.

Now That You Have Understood the Different Styles of Editing, I Want You To...

Analyze all three styles and choose the model that suits you the best. Carefully understand the pros and cons of every style and make an informed decision.

TRADITIONAL	SELF	HYBRID

9

WHY SHOULD I NEVER SELF-PUBLISH MY BOOK?

BIG IDEA: You have read about the cons of self-publishing in the previous chapter. This chapter will exclusively focus on why self-publishing might be a bad idea, especially if you are a first-time author.

If you have read the pros of self-publishing, you would have tilted toward this model. The freedom over your content, the higher royalty percentages, being yourself... Sure, they sound tempting. However, do not forget the cons! This chapter will, in detail, tell you why self-publishing is a bad idea in most circumstances. Just because self-publishing feels like all you want, do not make the mistake of assuming it will all be a cakewalk! Hiring freelancers and getting your work done in chunks may sound easy, but it definitely is not how it looks. Firstly, finding suitable freelancers is a task. Following up with them is another task.

Plus, if you do not like their work, you will have to keep switching or just do it yourself. In fact, it might get more expensive and might end up burning a hole in your pockets. That said, self-publishing is indeed a beautiful process.

Writing your content and managing things your way is all very satisfying. But the main factor that must be considered here is 'who should and who should not self-publish?' Those authors who already have a name and are writing their sixth or seventh book can self-publish. Those authors who have an excellent team of editors can self-publish. Those authors who are confident about their language and writing skills can self-publish. However, authors who are attempting to write a book for the first time and who do not have a team of professional editors, designers, and proofreaders, should not self-publish.

Here Are Some Other Pointers:

1. Since you are the only person on board, everything is up to you. Be it writing the book, hiring freelance editors and designers, or meeting deadlines—you are answerable to yourself. You are responsible for yourself. You cannot sit back and let the publisher handle everything. This might get tiring after a while.
2. Having no deadlines makes the entire process look out of place, and you might slack off and not get any work done. There are chances you might even lose interest in writing the book.
3. Publicizing and promoting the book is all on you. If you have good contacts and are experienced in managing an event, then you are safe. However, even if you do know everything, handling everything on your own is definitely stressful. Publishing houses have

been around for decades, and they know the market. They are all professionals. No matter how good a writer you are, publishing with the help of a publisher has its own perks.

4. Even with the most professional looking book, without publicity, no one will hear of it. After the time and money you have spent on production, it would be very foolhardy to skip publicity and social media campaigns.

5. You will have to personally reach out to media outlets and request them to review your book. Now, meeting media personnel is not easy; however, even if you do manage to catch hold of someone, having a PR team manage it for you is way easier and comfortable.

6. Self-publishing is a much quicker way of publishing, yes. But if you prefer quality work, it is good to have an editorial team by your side. Even if you are a good writer, it is always better to have a second set of professional eyes.

7. Self-publishing does not hold much value in the market. Often, self-publishers are not taken seriously. Why? Well, the only reason is you have not marketed your book properly.

8. If you are a first-time writer, **do not self-publish**. Although the entire process might be satisfactory, money is a major factor. As a self-publisher, all the up-front money comes right out of your pocket. If the book does not do well post publishing, you might find it difficult to recover your losses. Moreover, in such cases, if the author wants to approach a traditional publishing house for his/her next book, the publishing house might deny their project as their first book did

not do well. The reputation injury is another major disadvantage.

9. Since self-publishers have no agents by their side, planning the book launch, book promotion events, and book signing events will have to be handled by the author.

10. Lack of distribution is a major disadvantage of self-publishing. You are limited to selling through online book retailers unless you are willing to invest a lot more in your book and take a much higher risk. Distribution through bookstores is possible but expensive to achieve, and the risk is all on your side alone.

Now That You Know Why You Should Not Self-Publish, Do You Still Think Self-Publishing Is a Good Idea?

RESOURCE: VIDEO

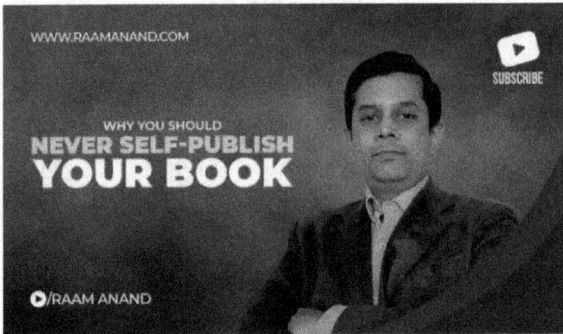

Visit: https://stardompublishing.com/evenmoreinfo/ -or- Scan this to play the video

10

SHOULD I PUT EVERYTHING I KNOW INTO MY FIRST BOOK?

BIG IDEA: Too much is too bad. However, too little is also not good. You must have the right balance. But how do you know how much is too much or how little is too little? Read this chapter to find your answers.

If you have started writing your book, you will definitely stumble upon these questions: "Should I be writing about everything I know?", "How much is too much?", "What exactly should I be writing about?", "What if the content I write is not enough?" These, and many more such doubts, will be on your mind. This is one of the reasons why the author must decide on their target audience before venturing into the project. For example, let us say you are writing a book on weight loss. As we know, in the present day, not everyone follows the same diet. While your content might be useful for someone who is a vegetarian, it might not be of any help to a strict vegan.

Therefore, choose your target audience and cater only to their needs. Make a mention of it on the book cover so that the reader can make an informed choice while buying the book. Do not aim for your book to be comprehensive. This is where many authors go wrong. In the process of trying to fit in everything you know, you might end up not doing justice to any of the topics. First time non-fiction authors make this common mistake of putting everything they know about a topic into their first book without even considering what the readers want. I once worked with an author, a business coach.

When I asked him about his target audience, he said, "everyone who is running a business." If someone says 'everyone' as their audience, they will reach no one in reality. It is imperative to think about the readers, their demographics, psychographics, and everything else even BEFORE you write your first chapter.

The ideal time for contemplation on this question would be before you even prepare the outline for your book. The outline system that we follow at Stardom Books is like the GPS navigation in your car. It will help you chart your journey from point A to point B by finding the best and the shortest route possible, without losing track and going around in circles, thereby wasting time and resources.

A book becomes a bestseller if the author's goals for the book aligns with the readers' goals. Here is a better way to think through this. Imagine a scenario wherein you have to present your topic to a group of people. They are already interested in the subject, and their attention span is about 4 hours. Now, figure out what you could teach them in these 4 hours. That presentation is what should go into your first book. You can always write more books or a series of books on your core topic, addressing different readers.

A good example is the book *Chicken Soup for the Soul*. After the initial launch of the book, it has now mushroomed into a gigantic series. There are more than 200 different titles (all with different ISBNs) in this series, each one targeted toward a specific readership.

Unless it is an encyclopedia or a 'list-type' book (e.g., A-Z lists, top 100 lists), you do not have to write a 1000-page book. Analyze the content you have, and most importantly, do not dump everything you know into one book. Perhaps you can think about a series of books or smaller chunks of your wisdom in each edition.

Here Are Some Ideas:

1. As I mentioned earlier, the first task is to decide on your target audience.

2. Research and list out the major topics that your readers might be interested in. Write about just that. Be clear about the message you want to convey.

3. The general rule of thumb is, one big idea per chapter and not more than a few big ideas per book. If you have more to share, think of a book series.

4. Talk about your passion and why you have targeted that particular group of audience. By narrowing down to a specific niche audience, you will actually increase the chances of selling more books because it resonates with the readers so well.

5. Addressing the question of 'why' you are writing this book and 'how' it will help the readers is important.

6. Again, having an outline definitely helps. It also helps you decide on what material should be included and in

which chapter it should go. So, create an outline first. It is like drafting a blueprint before constructing a building.

7. Have your introduction and conclusion ready. If you have these two in place, navigating through the rest of the chapters is not that difficult. Write what the reader must know, not what you want to say. People like reading short and to-the-point books, especially in the non-fiction category. If you beat around the bush and talk about extra content that does not relate to the book, the reader will definitely lose interest. So, plan accordingly.

8. There is no need for fillers in your book. However, a good editor knows how to 'enhance' the mundane teaching points by adding appealing edits into your book to make the content interesting to read.

Putting things in perspective, a good non-fiction author always identifies who the reader is. Your book is not for everyone; it cannot be for everyone. Being clear on this point will help you not only with your content but also with your marketing. By writing what YOU want to say instead of what the reader wants to read, you are just driving away your readers.

Fiction is different. You need to have backstories and additional scenarios there. People buy fiction books for entertainment. Hence, the bigger the better. However, in non-fiction, you need to talk about what you know and target a particular set of people.

Your non-fiction book should be clear on the 5Ws and 1H (Who, What, When, Where, Why, and How). **Now that you know how much is too much,** here is what I want you to do: Go on the Internet and research your target audience. Decide who you will be writing this book for. This will help you narrow down the content for your book. Once that is done, all you have to do is get started with the book!

"Either write something worth
reading or do something worth
writing."
- Benjamin Franklin

11

HOW TO CHOOSE THE RIGHT CHAPTERS FOR MY BOOK?

BIG IDEA: Deciding on chapters is indeed a difficult task. That is why I have dedicated an entire chapter to this topic. Go ahead, read on.

This is something all writers grapple with. Choosing the right chapters for your book is indeed a herculean task. You have several milestones ahead of you: choosing a topic, creating an outline, watering down the massive content, and organizing them the way you need, to name a few.

As an author, you will have to focus on every small detail in the book and come up with appropriate chapters. Why are we stressing so much on the importance of chapters? While buying a book, most people skim through the contents section. If your chapter headlines do not seem convincing, the reader might not be interested in your book.

However, if the chapter headline is catchy, the reader will be tempted to check out the chapter, and thereby, to buy your book. Getting just the chapter name right will not do the job. You will also have to make sure the content has relevance to the title. You will lose the reader if your chapter title and the chapter contents have no connection.

Therefore, the way you divide your non-fiction book into chapters and sections will have a direct impact on the reader's level of engagement. Chapters are signposts. They give your reader an idea of what is coming. Chapters help break up your material into manageable chunks for the reader. The first and foremost task is to come up with an outline. Creating an outline will help you organize your thoughts properly and give a structure to your upcoming book. Having a proper outline in place will also help you distribute content into different chapters accurately.

To create an outline, first list out all the points you want to discuss in your book. This list will help you understand the chronology of different topics and will make the process easier. At Stardom Books, our editors will work with you to create an outline for your book. As I mentioned earlier, do not try to fit everything in one chapter. Try keeping one main idea for each chapter. This will make sure you are not all over the place. If there is too much information, then expand the content over two chapters. Link the two chapters and put them under one section. Having chapters under different sections will also help the reader navigate his way through the book.

Now let us say you have too much content for one chapter. But you cannot expand it over another chapter as the content is not enough for a standalone chapter. What do you do in situations like these? The answer is simple—subdivide! Break the chapter into smaller sections and have subheadings. This will also help you title the chapters accurately.

Chapters can be constructed either to read sequentially (linear) or as reference material (non-linear or independent). For example, this book is non-linear, which means, you can open any chapter and start reading.

Here Are Some Frequently Asked Questions:

1. How do I make the chapter interesting?
2. How do I conclude a chapter? How creative should it be?
3. How to make sure the chapter brings out the accurate meaning?
4. How long should a chapter be?
5. When do I have a chapter break?
6. Should I title the chapter right away?

There is just one answer to all these questions: WRITE! Just keep writing. Your first draft will give you a clear idea on how the book might turn out. The draft will also help you edit and make the necessary changes to your book. Having questions is good, but do not let them bother you until you are done with your first draft. This is where the importance of editing comes into play. A book is not done in one go. It is more like a painting. The artist starts with a blank canvas and the final masterpiece is created in layers. Similarly, the first draft of a manuscript looks raw and unfinished. Over several rounds of editing and proofreading, it will begin to take form, and then after formatting, it will actually look like a book.

Titling Your Chapters:

Why are titles so important? Is it not the content inside the chapter that matters?

Well, not really. The chapter title provides a hint of what to expect within the chapter. Your title helps the reader consume the content he/she is looking for. Titles provide easy reference points for the reader. To give you an example, let us say Tom, an aspiring MBA student, picks up your book on business and leadership.

Tom is looking to find something on the efficient ways of managing a team. Now, your book about business can deal with several points from entrepreneurship to sales and marketing. If you have proper titles and sections, Tom can find the chapter he is looking for with just one quick look at the contents section.

If you title your chapters appropriately, it will help Tom understand what might be discussed in the chapter just by reading the title. The right title can help distinguish and provide a small glimpse into the chapter.

How Long Should the Chapter Be? How Do I Know When to End?

There is no set rule for chapter length. Just make sure to be clear and include only the required content. Also, make sure you have a good introduction and conclusion. The reader must have a clear idea about the topic discussed once he/she has completed reading that chapter. This should be your goal.

How Many Chapters Should I Have?

Again, this is subjective. If you prefer having subheadings and extra content in the same chapter, there will not be too many chapters in the book. However, if you like the idea of having several short chapters, then you can do so. In both cases, the word limit will remain the same.

The bottom line is this: choose whichever process suits you the best. But do not let this difficulty in coming up with chapters hinder your process of writing. Nothing should stop you from writing. If you are stuck coming up with a chapter title, do not worry. Just get your thoughts down on the paper and worry about structuring it later!

Remember, the basic rule of thumb is one big idea per chapter. And, for example, if this one big idea requires 5 steps to explain, then use sub-headings for each one of those steps. For example, Steven Covey's bestselling book, *The 7 Habits of Highly Effective People*, is split into seven chapters, one chapter for each habit.

Now That You Know How to Choose The Right Chapters for Your Book, Here is a Quick Assignment for You:

Are you clear on how to choose a chapter now? If not, read the chapter again. Choosing the right chapters helps you organize and structure your content. If you cross this phase, your book is on the right track.

RESOURCE: VIDEO

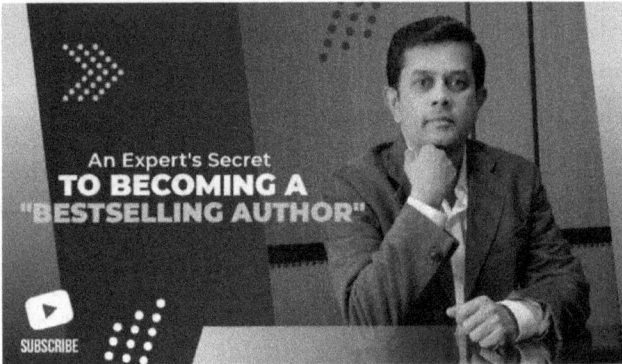

Visit: https://stardompublishing.com/evenmoreinfo/
-or-
Scan this to play the video

12

WHO WILL READ MY BOOK?

BIG IDEA: Negativity is bad. You have not even started writing your book yet. But I do not blame you. Most first-time authors face this question. All I can tell you is, Relax!

You are not alone. All bestselling authors have been through this phase, and they have all made it to the shore. You can too!

The simple answer to the question "who will read my book?" is "no one," unless you finish and publish your book. If 'wannabe' authors ask this question, there could be two different contexts: "WHO will read my book?"—This is a straightforward question that can be answered by figuring out the right audience and the topic your target audience wants to consume.

On the other hand, "Who will read MY book?" is a question that stems from low self-esteem or confidence issues. This is a dangerous and self-defeating question to ask. Why?

This particular question may bring down your spirits, and when that happens, you might start questioning the entire idea of writing a book. Even though you might have a message to share or a profound insight that can help people, you are doing a disservice to society by hesitating to tell that story or share those insights or perspectives. The information you are withholding could be a guiding light to someone. Why would you want to deny them that opportunity?

That said, one of the earliest hurdles writers can stumble over is comparing themselves with the authors who had the most significant impact on their lives. This train of thought is like going down a rabbit hole and should be avoided. The only way you can prevent yourself from getting stuck in this rut is to start writing. Pick up your pen or keyboard and start writing. Start telling your story. After all, it is your story and not theirs.

It can be a story that someone wants to read. Or, maybe, it is just a story you want to tell, a message you want to share, or a lesson you want to teach. And no one can do it better than you. Many people who are eligible to write a book do not even know this because they confuse writing a book with sharing their story in the form of a biography. They usually shoot down the idea of writing a book with a defeatist statement such as "I have not done much to write a book about myself," or "I do not have a lot to write about," or even, "I am not old enough to write a book!"

There are many such reasons and excuses people give for not deciding to publish a book. However, the underlying cause is almost always either a lack of courage or ignorance of how to approach 'writing a book.'

Previously, we have discussed the various excuses made by people for failing to get started on a book. While some do not find the time and complain about the lack of attention, many others hesitate because of a fear of failure. They have a lot of questions: What will happen once my book gets published? What if no one picks it up? How will my career get impacted if my book fails? This fear of criticism and failure stops many from embarking on this beautiful journey of writing a book.

"There are so many books out there on this subject already. Why would people pick up my book?" Well, this is a serious question, and it needs to be addressed. Yes, there will be many other books on the same topic in the market. They might even be written by established authors. However, this should not take your focus away. So what if there are many other books on the same topic? It is up to you to show how creative you can get with your book. Think of your book as a teaching aid. What would you teach other people about your topic(s)?

Another crucial factor I would like to stress on is comparing oneself to other authors. As I said earlier, everyone has a different writing style, and everyone has a different story to tell. Why would you compare yourself, a debutant book writer, to an already established author? Every renowned author has been where you are right now. Everyone has felt this fear. Those who have made it have faced their fears and achieved their goals. So, it is up to you. Will you give in to your fear of "Who will read my book?" and back out, or work smart, get support, and turn your dream into reality?

Your only way out is to start writing. There is no backing out now. You have committed to writing a book. So, do not let anything scare you. Think about what a good role model you will be to the younger generation if you make it and successfully publish your book! There might be a scared kid somewhere in the world, just like you, and this book might help that kid overcome her fears. Think about all the good karma! I am not saying writing is easy; it definitely is not. In fact, it is easier to talk. But writing is not impossible either.

Once you get the hang of writing, you will not want to stop. So, do not worry. The first step is to download your thoughts onto a sheet of paper or a word document. Collect all the necessary content for your book. The next step is to structure them and put them into a book format (organizing the content under different chapters and sections, as per the outline). Once that is done, your first draft of the manuscript is ready. Now, do not make the mistake of reading your first draft and assuming it to be your end product. NO! The first draft is supposed to be bad.

That is how you improve and learn. Writing and deleting is part of the process. In the end, when the final product is out, you will realize that every draft was worth your time. Now the next question is "What if I am the only one who likes my book?" This is a genuine concern. My advice is, convert this question into a thought and explore it. Think about why people might or might not like your book. Now, addressing the elephant in the room, "What will happen to my career if my book is a flop?" Well, if this thought ever comes to you, just push it away, and lock it in some corner of your brain. You are writing this book because you are well versed in what you do. You know stuff better than others, and you are writing a book to help them.

So, when your book's purpose is to help people navigate their lives, why would it be a flop? It won't be! Further, at Stardom Books, our authors do not write a book first and then look for readers. It is the other way around. We first research the readers, their issues, their problems, and what keeps them awake at three in the morning, and then choose a topic that aligns with both the author's goals and the readers' goals. This way, your book project is engineered or designed to resonate with a known group of people, even before you write your first sentence.

You might say, "Yes, I know my stuff, and I am good at what I do. However, people do not recognize me by my name. Why would anyone pick up a book written by an unknown author?" Okay, valid question, again. But, tell me this. How did these famous authors become 'famous'? Do you think they have had no failures? Do you think they were all famous the very moment they wrote a book? In her 2008 Harvard University commencement speech, renowned author J K Rowling said, "I was the biggest failure I knew and as poor as one can be in England without having to be homeless." It was in this very hopeless phase of her life that she started writing! Nobody knew her back then. However, look at the stardom she has achieved today! Whenever you have doubts about your writing skills, or you are facing a fear of people not reading your books, just look up a few famous authors and read their life history.

You will definitely be inspired. Now, let us imagine the worst case. Let us say you publish your book, and it does not do that well. It is no biggie. Look at *Lord of the Flies* by William Golding. Before it got published, this book was rejected 20 times, and one of the reviewers called it "absurd and uninteresting fantasy which was rubbish and dull." Well, try telling this to the top libraries and book publishers now. Another golden example is Stephen King. He was absolutely broke when *Carrie* got accepted. It is said that Stephen disliked the story so much that he threw away his original manuscript into the garbage! So, never give up. Let me share another big idea here. You do not have to invent any new thing or make an earth-shattering discovery to write a book. Non-fiction or business books have a purpose—teach or spread a message or share some insights. That is all you need.

For example, in one of the most famous books in the business category, *The 7 Habits of Highly Effective People*, author Stephen Covey shares the seven habits and if you observe carefully, none of these habits were completely new. It is not like people did not know any of those habits.

However, the book became a big hit because Stephen put all the seven most useful habits together and created a framework around them. He gave examples and his own insights for each one of them. He laid out the best practices and the guide to each one of those seven habits. You can do the same. I am sure you can think of at least seven big ideas about your area of expertise that you can teach other people. That is all you need to get started.

To Help You Keep Focused, Here are Some Tips:

1. Do not compare yourself to other authors. You are a different person, and you have your own voice. Identify that. If you do want to compare, compare yourself to a previous version of yourself when you were far away from the idea of publishing a book. Look at how much you have grown! Give yourself the liberty to make mistakes.

2. Do not edit while you write. The first draft is supposed to be bad. Just write and put everything out on the table.

3. Writing a book is cathartic. Prepare yourself before you start writing, and make up your mind to not quit in between. Write your book your way. It is your voice. However, be sure to not deviate from your target

audience. As I mentioned earlier, explore a new angle to the same topic and give your book a unique angle that is new to the readers.

Before I wrap up this chapter, I want to answer the question "Who will read my book?" one last time. Many people might, or it might just be your family and friends. But someone will definitely read it. However, if you do not write at all, no one, I repeat, NO ONE will read it, ever.

Now That You Are Clear on Not Letting the Fear of "Who Will Read My Book" Get in Your Way, Here is a Quick Assignment for You:

Take a sheet of paper or open your journal. Think about five pieces of advice you can give to others on topics such as Career, Relationships, Health, Wealth, Money, Work, and Business. Go ahead and add your own topics and brainstorm five or more tips, ideas, or pieces of advice you can give on each topic. What five things can you teach? What five steps do you advise? What five questions can you answer? You get the drift, do you not? In under thirty minutes, you will be able to come up with dozens, if not hundreds of ideas. This list could become the starting point of your next book!

A great book should leave you with many experiences, and slightly exhausted at the end. You live several lives while reading.

- William Styron

13

DO I HAVE THE KNOWLEDGE TO WRITE A BOOK?

BIG IDEA: The content in the pages of a non-fiction book is not about knowledge. It is about focus. You get the reader's attention to focus on a specific problem, issue, or insight.

Let us start by understanding the terms 'knowledge' and 'wisdom'. Many people confuse knowledge with wisdom as they are closely related, but the two words are quite different from each other. Knowledge is a collection of facts and related information. Wisdom, on the other hand, is an amalgamation of knowledge and experiences into insights or perspectives. In other words, knowledge is merely a tool, and wisdom is the craft in which the tool is used. (*"The Wisdom Hierarchy"*) If you understand this difference, you will also know why it is essential to differentiate the two correctly. Any person who possesses the diligence and patience to spend some time in this age of the Internet can quickly amass knowledge in whichever field he or she chooses.

Google has done a great job at putting together an incredible amount of facts and information. We are in the age of information overload. But having a knife and knowing how to wield it are two entirely different propositions. Consider a chef and a thief. How we view the knife in these two different situations depends on the user and not the tool. Sadly, our history features a lengthy list of the wrongs caused by knowledgeable, well-intentioned people who lacked wisdom. In contrast, wisdom is perceived as morally right. Why?

Albert Einstein said it best, "Wisdom is not a product of schooling but of the lifelong attempt to acquire it." So, we gain knowledge but glean wisdom through our experiences. It can be a lengthy and arduous process, but it will teach the seeker patience and humility. It is extremely rare to see a person unchanged by such a quest.

When one finally uncovers a connection or insight that one believes can be a universally applicable 'truth,' it often inspires awe and appreciation. "Knowledge comes, but wisdom lingers," wrote Alfred, Lord Tennyson. Truth will accompany a person for the rest of his or her life. Wisdom does not dictate or demand obedience. It does not threaten. The practitioner obeys out of his or her own volition because of his or her beliefs. Knowledge is the aggregation of the facts and information that you have learned or experienced. It is to be aware of the circumstances and have the data about them.

To put it simply, knowledge is the data that we acquire through observation, investigation, research, and study. Wisdom is the ability to decipher the data collected and determine which aspects are true, lasting, and applicable to your life. It is the ability to apply the knowledge you have learned to the grander scheme of life. It is also insightful to know the meaning or the reason behind why something is the way it is and what it means to your life.

Knowledge is to know about managing your money, budgeting, spending, and saving. Wisdom is to understand how money impacts the quality of your life and your future. Knowledge is learning how to tell a story and using that skill to cultivate a livelihood.

Wisdom is expressing your passion through writing and understanding that art is a form of communication that touches the lives of others. Let me break this down for you. Can you give me a piece of advice you would give to someone in the area of your expertise?

Let us say a high school student asks you for advice on 'fitness.' Would you be able to share with them a life lesson or two? If you said 'yes' to the question above, you have everything you need to write a book. A non-fiction book is just an extension of your advice with facts, figures, statistics, and stories that support your suggestions. It is impossible to lead an utterly uninteresting life. Well, okay, it is possible, but it is tough.

However, if you said 'no', fret not. None of our authors are professional writers. They are just people with high aspirations with a message to share. Most often, it is not the lack of content that authors have to struggle with. The bigger struggle is to decide what goes into the book.

Most first-time authors try to put everything they know into their book because they want to make it the 'best' book ever. That would be true only if the end product is going to be an encyclopedia. For a regular non-fiction book, all you need is about 40,000 to 60,000 words. This will result in a decent book between 150 and 200 pages in length, when completed.

As I mentioned earlier, be clear on how much is too much content. Be clear on what your reader wants to learn from you. Having clarity about this will help you structure your book. It is also essential to map out your reader's journey, plan your book before you start to write, and get clear on where you are taking your readers.

Lastly, remember this, you do not need to 'prepare' to write a book. Of course, you will need to research and read up, but do not hold back from writing just because you are not prepared. Start and things will eventually fall into place, like magic!

Now, Quick Assignment:

Do you think you have enough knowledge to write a book? Yes? Then what are you waiting for? No? Well, then gather more information. Dig deeper. Challenge yourself and learn about all that is needed to write a book on your chosen topic.

RESOURCE: VIDEO

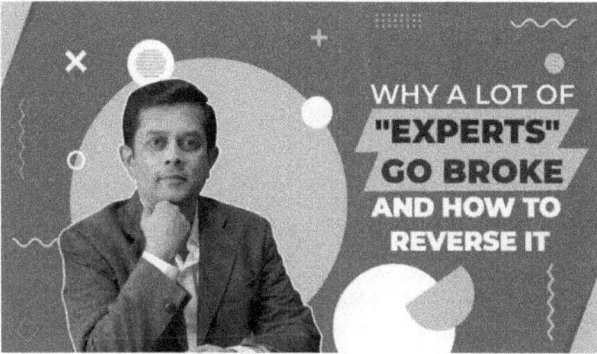

Visit: https://stardompublishing.com/evenmoreinfo/
-or-
Scan this to play the video

Books were my pass to personal
freedom.

- Oprah Winfrey

14

DO I NEED A COACH TO HELP ME BECOME AN AUTHOR? HOW TO CHOOSE ONE?

BIG IDEA: Coaching has been known to boost confidence, improve project performance, and build effective communication skills.

Like any other big challenge, writing a book is a significant milestone. So, having a good coach who can guide you through the way might help you set clear goals for your book. A coach will help you overcome the various hurdles of book writing and save you from losing sight of the end result. The world's highest achievers have coaches for various areas like fitness, business, meditation, spiritual, finance, high-performance, parenting, communication, voice training, management, fashion, and many others.

Having a Coach Has Many Benefits:

1. Developing a roadmap for success with clear milestones so that you reach those goals.
2. Creating a system or a plan for taking up the journey of writing and publishing your book.
3. Evaluating your progress vis-a-vis the formulated plan at regular intervals and make any changes, if needed, according to the situation.
4. Organizing and developing your book or book proposal.
5. Giving you simple and easy-to-use plans, templates, or tools to help you expedite the launching of your book.
6. Expanding your author platform.
7. Developing a compelling promotion plan for your book.

That said, choosing a coach is not an easy task. You will consider many things. To help you, here are seven critical factors to consider when you are hiring ANY coach:

- **Experience/Education:**

Are they qualified and educated to help you succeed? Are their education and experience forged in the realities of the marketplace? Or are they just regurgitating the content they learned from someone else?

If I were to look for an expert to learn from, I would always choose the person who has worked in the particular field and who will, therefore, have valuable and viable insights to share. So, if you are looking to hire the services of a coach to help publish your book, you should look for someone who has excelled in all three areas—reading (someone who reads a lot of books), writing (who has already written their own books), and publishing (who has published other peoples' books).

- **Facing Challenges Head-On:**

Enquire if your prospective coach or mentor has dealt with his/her share of challenges. These need not have been in the same field as yours, but make sure your coach has been where you are now. If your mentor/coach has had it easy, you might have difficulty bonding with them. Why is this important? Well, a coach who has gone through life hurdles will help you see the world as it is and prepare you for all sorts of challenges life might throw at you.

- **Verifiable Results:**

Have they created or produced the same results you want to manifest, or do they 'just teach this stuff' from reading books on those topics? Would it not be better to learn from those people who have travelled on the same path that you now want to traverse? Is it not better to learn from those who can walk their talk and who have 'been there done that'?

Your coach should be a role model for you in terms of their success or have a track record of genuinely making a positive difference in the world and helping their clients. Their success will motivate you to reach for the same heights.

Another point to note here is that your coach should be successful in terms of what you think success is. After all, success is relative and unique to every individual.

- **Values Alignment:**

Are your values aligned with the coach's? For example, you might be a fun-loving, upbeat, and laid-back person and your coach more like an old-school drillmaster. In this situation, you might struggle to understand and apply the practices and strategies they impart to you. While this may be an extreme example, you should be aware that even the slightest hint of incompatibility between your values and your coach's can cause this process of writing your book to be knocked askew.

- **Program Content:**

Analyze the methods your coach intends to practice. Will you enjoy implementing the strategies he/she prescribes? Will you find the process that he/she wants you to subscribe to as fun and authentic? Make an informed decision. Having a coach you do not vibe with is a bad idea, and it will only compromise the quality of your book.

- **Satisfied Clients:**

Who are their clients? Are they happy with their results? Check for their testimonials and reviews. Make sure to ask around before committing to the person.

- **Learning Structure:**

Analyze and review the methods your coach uses. Are you being benefited? Are his/her teachings and ways aiding you to reach your goal? Having said that, do not rush and make a hasty decision. Some things take time.

So, review your coach after spending a month or two. If it still does not work for you, then you need a different coach. I encourage you to note and save these pointers. Have it as a checklist. Use it to evaluate your options and choose the one who checks off all the pointers.

Complete This Sentence:

The key factors I look for in a publishing coach include

_____

_____

_____

_____

15

HOW WILL I PROFIT
FROM MY OWN BOOK?

BIG IDEA: A book is a business asset and it should be created in such a way that it produces both direct and indirect returns for the author.

We have explored how a book can indirectly bring you plenty of return on investment (RoI) by generating leads. In tangible terms, authors profit from the royalties from the sale of their books. If you were to publish your book via the traditional publishing model adopted by 'pre-Amazon' publishing houses, you would receive a royalty of a paltry 7% to 15%. If you were to opt for the self-publishing route, you would keep all the proceeds from the book's sales. Hybrid publishing is the middle ground. This model is so powerful because it brings the best of both worlds; it will fetch the author 50% to 100%

royalties along with the ability to use the book publisher's resources, guidance, and expertise.

Let us have a deeper look into how much an author can profit out of writing a book. Firstly, we have to keep in mind that no two authors will earn the same amount of profit on their books. It depends on your authenticity, writing, genre, experience, size of the audience, and also the number of books published and sold.

Now, authenticity increases as you write and publish more books, and the same goes for your size of audience and experience. So, the best bet to make profits out of your book is to write and publish frequently. You can use your book as a marketing strategy.

Here Are Some Ways You Will Be Benefited from Your Book:

You can use many weapons in a marketing campaign, but a book authored by you is incredibly powerful. Your book will be effective when it is centered around your business. Books are extremely useful when it comes to generating leads for your business or profession. If you are doubtful of this fact, look no further than Tony Robbins, who has used books as a tool to drive multitudes of people to attend his workshops and events.

Do not think of the returns on a book purely in tangible terms. You could make a decent return on investment (RoI) when you see the book's royalties fill up your bank account, but do not discount the intangible returns. Sometimes the intangible returns can be substantial and of far more worth than the royalties earned from the book sales.

1. Paid Speaking

By publishing a book, you are telling people about your expertise. You are putting yourself on the map. This will open up a lot of doors, including paid speaking. If there is a conference or a talk being held on the topic you have authored a book on, you will be invited as a speaker to those events, and this will fetch you a lot of fame. One thing leads to another, and you will end up with numerous speaking assignments, thanks to your book. Attending these talks will also help expand your contacts.

Books are the gateway to speaking engagements and becoming keynote speakers.

2. Promote A Facility Or Conference

You can use your book to promote a facility or an event. For instance, the founders of the Kentucky Entrepreneur Hall of Fame wanted to get more attention for their cause. So, they wrote *Unbridled Spirit*, a book about all the famous Kentuckians who started great companies.

3. Consulting Services

Just like you get invited for talks, people will approach you for consulting services. Once you get recognized as an expert and a published author in a particular field, opportunities will come knocking on your door.

Your book will tell people about your work, what it would be like to partner with you, and how you would be able to help them. A book makes your life easier by telling people what they have to know about you.

4. Freelance Gigs

Let us say you are someone who does not want to work for others. Well, everyone wants to be an entrepreneur these days. As the joke goes, "What do people do in their free time? They start-up!"

If you are an entrepreneur, write a book on the aim of your company and the history of how it all started, and through your book, make people understand the difference your company will bring to society.

Convince them as to why they should approach you. Once you have a published book, people will be familiar with the company's name, and thus, they will choose you over several other companies in the same business. You will be considered credible.

5. Change Careers

Even if you don't have your own business or not pursuing entrepreneurial aspirations, a book can help you substantially advance your career, either within your current organization or by helping you switch your career completely.

6. Attract High Net-Worth Clients

If you are in business with high net-worth professionals, you know how difficult they can be. Having a book makes that job much easier. An example is Alex Andrawes, a high-end wine broker who helps people invest in fine wines. He was successful before writing a book, but after he published his book on investing in fine wines, he doubled his inbound leads and tripled his highest net worth clients—in only a year. Another example would be Nick Tarascio. He owns an airplane brokerage business. There are very few people who can afford to buy an airplane, and he used his book to help him attract and close numerous buyers.

7. Generating Leads

You can give away your valuable book for free (or a small fee) in exchange for the contact details of interested buyers. Let us take the example of this very book: If you are reading the print version, it is likely that you would have only paid for shipping and handling. I gave away this book to know the details of people interested in bringing out their books. This is a win–win situation for both of us.

Let us revisit the example of Tony Robbins. He gave away his book *Money* to tens of thousands of people all over the world for the very same reason. He could have followed the conventional way of selling books online and offline, and he would still have had people buying the book at face value. However, he would never have been able to build a database of interested prospects quickly and effectively, using this model.

8. Sell Physical Products

It can be a common sight to see pamphlets and flyers promoting products on the street. Any profitable business will have a brochure listing their products to show a prospective client. The natural reaction to brochures as sales material is predictable, but your products could gain a greater legitimacy when it is listed in a book. It would be beneficial to convert all your sales brochures into one comprehensive book with relevant additional information like pictures, articles, customer reviews, illustrations, etc.

9. Video/Information Course

If you have an online video or information course, look no further than a book to drive customers to these courses. Your book could promote the online course and encourage your readers to sign up for the course. Books become a crucial offline marketing tool to sell your content online. The learning and development industry and the people who promote such programs can benefit greatly and build their expert-empire around a book. In this field, books are very powerful and help in positioning and attracting interested prospects to their workshops and events.

10. Promote Services

Like discussed earlier, books give a greater sense of legitimacy to your products than a brochure or a flyer ever could. This is true of even the service industry. Books demand greater respect from the reader, and a book promoting your services will attract people more than a website or a pamphlet. When you write a book about the problems your audience is facing and the obvious solutions to those problems, you will start attracting the right people who are actually looking for such solutions. Books are great at drawing leads because a book is a convenient, risk-free, entry-level commitment that most prospects use to 'test' you before they seek you out.

11. Paid Masterminds/Community

A properly written user manual can bring in really focused participants to paid masterminds and community initiatives—a great strategy to find and keep interested participants instead of advertising.

12. Raise Money For Causes

People buy books for worthwhile and charitable causes and, in some cases, even donate their books to other people. One of the more unique ways by which you can promote a non-profit or bring a cause to everyone's attention is by writing a book about it. This strategy has not been ignored and is actually in ascendance today. You can also raise capital for start-ups.

Imagine you are invited to pitch your idea to a group of investors. It is a natural part of the proceedings to find a few other start-ups competing for the attention of this group. They bring their business cards while you give your internationally published book (autographed, of course) to each investor. On the other hand, it is also important that you spend time understanding the readers' buying habits in your genre and customize your book accordingly.

Here Are Some More Tips on How to Profit from Your Book:

1. Choose Hybrid Publishing

Understand all three publishing styles, note down the pros and cons for each, and make an informed decision.

2. Understand Your Audience

I have said this before, and I will repeat this. Be clear on your target audience and focus on catering to their needs. Do your research on their wants and customize your book accordingly. Make the book relatable.

3. Write Every Day And Hasten The Process

Do not just sit on the idea. Execute the plan. Write every day and make sure to get your book out in the market as soon as possible.

4. Socialize

Just writing a book is not enough. Talk about it. Get on social media platforms or let people in your family and those in your circle of friends know that you are writing a book. This has two advantages. Firstly, you will be showered with inputs: you can choose what you want to consider. And next, it leads to word of mouth.

The marketing has started even before you are done with the book. While this might pressurize some, look on the bright side. Since people will be talking about your book, you will stay on course and finish it on time!

Additionally, create an email list and mail people updates about your book, what they can expect out of the book, the launch date, etc. Keep your readers in the loop. A good example is how James Canfield and Mark Victor Hansen, authors of the *Chicken Soup for the Soul* series of books, did their promotional activities that led to the extraordinary success of their books.

5. Publish Your Book In Series

Let us assume you are writing a book on 'Environmental Conservation.' Now, this is a vast topic. Instead of cramming everything into one single book, you could write a series of three books, writing in detail on every sub-topic in a separate book. For instance, your first book can be about the man-made activities that damage the environment. The second book can be about the damage done and the consequences. Finally, your third book can be about the measures and various initiatives that need to be taken to tackle environmental degradation. This way, you will have three books under your belt, and you will be considered an expert on the topic, thanks to the detailed explanations. Lastly, you will have to commit to the writing process. If you plan to make money and profit from your book for a long time, you will have to commit to it. Sure, even a single book can fetch you a lot of fame and recognition. But if you want to stay in business for a longer time, you will have to keep writing and publishing books.

FILL IN THE GRID:

Direct returns from my book	Indirect returns from my book

If there is a book that you want to read, but it hasn't been written yet, you must be the one to write it.

- Toni Morrison

16

WHY SHOULD I PUBLISH MY BOOK RIGHT NOW?

BIG IDEA: Is there a right time to write a book? Find out in this chapter.

We only have one life. It might sound a bit clichéd, but it bears repeating. We do not live forever. Our time in this life has an end date. So, we need to be clear about how we want to spend our time. If you have the desire to write a book, do not look for external factors to force your hand. There is only one right time to write a book—that time is now. There is no better opportunity to share your thoughts, passions, and story with the world. Do not leave this knock on your door unanswered. Inherently, writing is a thoughtful activity that requires deep introspection. The process of writing will demand that you turn your thoughts inward. This is also an exercise that forces you to be honest with yourself. And thus, through writing, you will realize and recognize what really matters to you.

Writing a book is also an exercise to test the strength of your resolve and willpower. The act of committing to a writing project might seem simple, but only when you see it through, will you find out the depths of your rigor and discipline.

As discussed earlier, writing keeps you in touch with your values, motivations, and thoughts. It can shine as a beacon providing direction to your life. As a bonus, writing is cheaper than therapy on any day! To understand this better, let us take an analogy of parenthood. You may weigh all the possible pros and cons of becoming a parent.

You could also read any number of books with expert views on parenting. You can even gauge whether you are financially, physically, and emotionally ready to become a parent. However, none of this will ever make it clear to you how challenging, amazing, and enriching your life will be once you really become a parent. These feelings and experiences are similar to what you will feel like as an author. Only when you can usher a new creative life into the world through your book will you realize the manifold ways writing a book will better your life. Once you experience this feeling, you will be left wondering why you did not do it sooner.

I am here to tell you that you should write a book, and you should do it right now. When you have authored a book, it significantly boosts your professional authority no matter what it is about. You have done something that very few people can claim to have become or accomplished: you are an author. Take your time and do it right, but do not hold off for the 'perfect timing'—that perfect timing is, after all, the present.

Readers need time to discover a new author, and if you keep waiting for the right time, it might never come. However, that does not mean you have to rush into it. Take your time, but make sure you do not take too much time. Once you complete the first draft of your book, start editing. Go over your edits closely. Make revisions. Sit with your new book cover and make sure you are happy with it. This process takes time. But that should not be your excuse to delay publishing your book.

Many people think they have to wait for a long time to write their own book, but that might be the worst mistake that could actually hurt them and their business or profession. I get it. Everyone says that you have to wait long enough to gather enough wisdom to write a book. It is easy to believe that.

But the real question is... WHY write a book and not WHEN to write it... Because it is not just about sharing your personal story or journey; it is about opening up new opportunities by reaching the right people. When it comes to leadership, you will agree that one must take up responsibility as soon as possible and show up as their best self and lead by example, right? It is leadership 101.

As a person in a leadership role, you already know that you should tell the world about what you stand for, your vision, and what you believe in this world. That is what makes you a leader and keeps you up there. You bring hope and help to your followers. When you communicate your values, ideas, insights, and perspectives, people will be able to resonate with your thoughts because they now understand your message. They understand you because *you* understand them.

Great movements were started in the world because the leaders communicated his or her message to their followers in a simple way. Many great movements also ended with the fall of their leaders because the message was not carried forward by the successors in the same way. It is your vision. It is your story. It is your narrative... And that is called personal branding.

What is it that you stand for? What do you believe in? Who do you believe in? Your grand vision... What is it? Answers to all these questions, when communicated in an easy-to-understand format, will help you connect with your people at more deeper levels.

RESOURCE: VIDEO

Visit: https://stardompublishing.com/evenmoreinfo/
-or-
Scan this to play the video

17

HOW MANY BOOKS CAN I WRITE AND PUBLISH?

BIG IDEA: Nobody said you will have to write just one book!

There is no one-size-fits-all answer to this question. J D Salinger wrote *The Catcher in the Rye,* and Margaret Mitchell wrote *Gone with the Wind* and never published a book again. Harper Lee published *Go Set A Watchman* 55 years after she wrote *To Kill a Mockingbird.* Then there is the example of the *Chicken Soup for the Soul* series of books, with hundreds of titles. So, there is no definite answer to this question.

Jack Canfield and Mark Victor Hansen, two motivational speakers, joined hands and collected true motivational stories shared by their audience. They published these stories in a book called *Chicken Soup for the Soul.* Interestingly, their work was rejected by numerous major publishers in New York City.

But then, a small self-help publishing company in Florida, HCI, accepted the manuscript.

Their book was a runaway success, and they found new contributors. These contributors came from different demographic areas and addressed various topics like growth, maturity, loss, grief, survival, etc. Canfield and Hansen published successful sequels to the book and also branched out to demographic-specific titles like *Chicken Soup for the Teenage Soul, Chicken Soup for the Cancer-Survivor's Soul, Chicken Soup for the Pet-Lover's Soul, Chicken Soup for the Mother's Soul, Chicken Soup for the Traveler's Soul,* and many others. As of 2020, the series has over 250 titles.

Another great example is the *Rich Dad Poor Dad* series of books. This series features 16 titles, but they all carry the same core message. However, they all are tailored to cater to different communities with specific examples and stories for them to relate to.

These examples perfectly illustrate why you should not limit yourself with the question "How many books can I write and publish?" The straightforward and possibly the simplest answer is that you can write as many books as you want. However, getting started and publishing your first book is critical to finding the answer for yourself. When you bring out your first book, you would have experienced the challenges and the associated results of the process. Once you are armed with this knowledge and experience, you can set goals to write as many books as you want.

The quantity of books you want to write primarily depends on the quality of the content you want to share. Thus, the content of the first non-fiction book must have the scope and potential for further exploration. It also depends on how long you take to publish your first book. This is where I can help you. In my 'Bestseller Author Bootcamp,' I teach many 'rapid book creation' frameworks that can be used to create interesting and successful books quickly. Some of our authors have created up to four books within a year, and all of them became bestsellers.

As I have mentioned earlier, typically, a non-fiction business book is about 150–200 pages in length and is produced in a standard 8.5 inches by 5.5 inches printed format. This is about 40,000 to 60,000 words of content.

With the 'rapid book creation' framework that I teach in my publishing programs, you can easily whip out a fully structured book in about 25 hours of dedicated effort (usually spread over a few weeks).

So how many books should you write in a year? Write as many as you like. Write to the best of your ability while taking care of the sort of writing you want to do. It would be best to find where your limits are and where your capabilities lie and work within those parameters. Write the kind of books you would want to buy and read. If you are going to write four books a year, that is excellent.

If you want to write a book every eleven years, that is very good as well. Most writers, I believe, will fall in between these two extremes. That will work. Worldwide statistics say that only 1% of the population will actually write and publish a book. Do you want to be the first person in your peer group or family, or company to write a book? Then, start right away.

So, how many books should you write in a year? As many as you like, and as many as you can do, within your ability for the sort of writing you want to do. You need to discover what your capabilities are and then work within them.

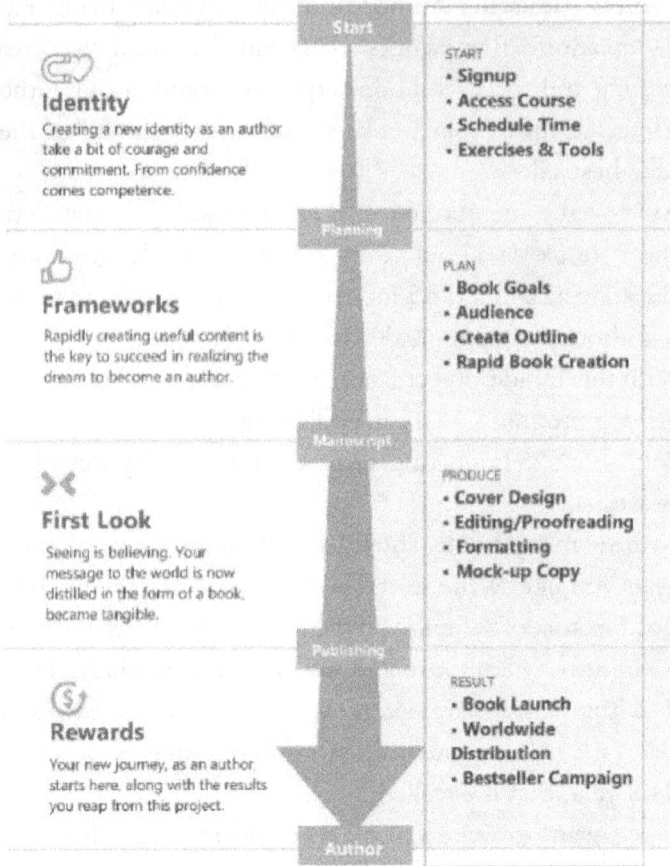

	Start	START
Identity		• Signup
Creating a new identity as an author take a bit of courage and commitment. From confidence comes competence.		• Access Course • Schedule Time • Exercises & Tools
	Planning	PLAN
Frameworks		• Book Goals
Rapidly creating useful content is the key to succeed in realizing the dream to become an author.		• Audience • Create Outline • Rapid Book Creation
	Manuscript	PRODUCE
First Look		• Cover Design
Seeing is believing. Your message to the world is now distilled in the form of a book, became tangible.		• Editing/Proofreading • Formatting • Mock-up Copy
	Publishing	RESULT
Rewards		• Book Launch
Your new journey, as an author starts here, along with the results you reap from this project.		• Worldwide Distribution • Bestseller Campaign
	Author	

Assignment:

Take a sheet of paper and write down all the big ideas on separate columns. Let us say, you want to share 5 big ideas. Write them down in 5 columns. Then, under each big idea, write down the points you want to share or teach. Now you have a grid. In your book, you can go either 'shallow and wide' or 'narrow and deep', which means, you can just focus on the top one or two levels (rows) under each big idea or go really deep into each one. If it became too big for one book, you have a series in your hand. Another strategy is to customize the core message to specific audiences, creating a series of books, for example, the *Chicken Soup for the Soul* series of books (there are 250 titles).

RESOURCE: VIDEO

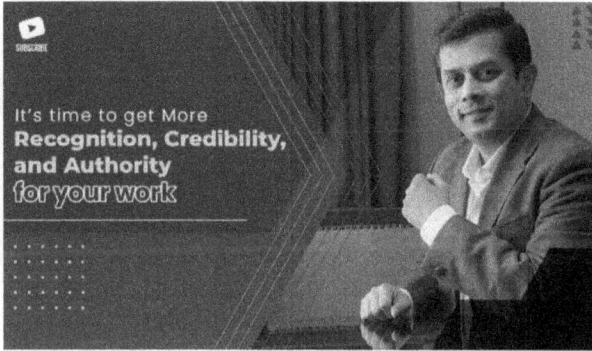

Visit: https://stardompublishing.com/evenmoreinfo/
-or-
Scan this to play the video

Writing comes from reading, and reading is the finest teacher of how to write.

- Annie Proulx

18

SHOULD I PUBLISH ONLY IN MY COUNTRY OR WORLDWIDE?

BIG IDEA: Publishing your book internationally has many perks. Some of them are discussed in this chapter. The bottom line here is, if you want a global audience and wider reach, you must publish internationally.

The question essentially is whether you want your book to be read by people who belong only to your country or you want a global reader base. The answer will be evident by the topic of your book. If your book is on how to crack a local university entrance test, naturally, most of your readers will be local. On the other hand, if your book is of a more general topic of interest, like personal development or self-help, you may find a more varied reader base, spread across the world. However, with the ease and convenience of global travel today, I would always recommend publishing an international edition of your book.

It adds a greater perceived value to the book and the author because of the International ISBN, backed by an established publisher. Another benefit of publishing an international edition is that your book becomes far more accessible to international readers. Your book will be stocked and sold by local retailers in different countries. Readers will be able to purchase the book using their local currency. They will not have to worry about shipping charges.

Consider this example: You are one of the leading psychologists in India and you have been recognized worldwide for your contributions to the field. You have authored a book on mental health. Thanks to your popularity, the book has received a lot of attention. Now, you publish the book within the country. The readers abroad will have to ship your book from one country to another. The readers will find this expensive as the cost of shipping might surpass the price of the book. Although the book deserves a global audience, it might end up being restricted to the local reading community. At the end of the day, although the book has the potential to affect and influence many readers, the reach was restricted as it was not published internationally. Therefore, you are severely limiting your book's potential by not publishing internationally.

Authors will have to make sure their books are available in some of the leading bookstores in different countries to widen their reach. That said, publishing your book in the UK and the US is definitely competitive. With many book fairs and other events in recent times, the market has opened up to everyone. You would be aware of the prestigious London Book Fair. It is a large book-publishing trade fair held annually, usually in April, in London, England. This fair hosts agents and publishers from around the world, and this can help you widen your audience. Therefore, you do not have to worry about not having an audience anymore.

Know this: The key is the voice of your book. If it is constrained to only your community or if the ideology is restricted to a single community, then your book's chances of being welcomed by a global audience are less.

Now, I agree that I have discussed the importance of being clear on your target audience in earlier chapters. Yes, having a target audience and catering to their needs is essential. However, if you aim to publish internationally, you will have to adjust your target audience slightly and modify the book's voice and content accordingly.

When you have your book listed with a retailer overseas, the chances of you being noticed is higher. Another important point about overseas marketing is your book cover and title. Whenever a reader picks up a book, one of the first things they look at is the book cover. If that is not appealing, they will not even bother giving it a second look. So, keeping your target audience in mind, do a bit of research and customize the book cover and title according to the region. You can hire freelance designers or ask the publishing house you are working with to help you with these details.

E-books Are Another Way to Go!

E-books are another way to market your book internationally. Several surveys support this. One of the surveys conducted by the Chinese Academy of Press and Publication showed that majority of the adults in the country use their phones to read books, and this number keeps increasing every year. Many young users prefer e-books in recent times, and this is proving to be true in all countries. The

US, India, Germany, South Korea, the UK, and many other countries have embraced e-books.

However, other countries like Belgium and France still prefer actual printed books. So, a good idea would be to have both printed editions and e-books. Why am I stressing so much about publishing internationally? Well, without the right means of reaching that audience, rich content can never be fully appreciated. If you want more and more readers to read and understand your book and share your view of the world, you have to focus on expanding your audience, and the best way to do that is publishing internationally.

RESOURCE: VIDEO

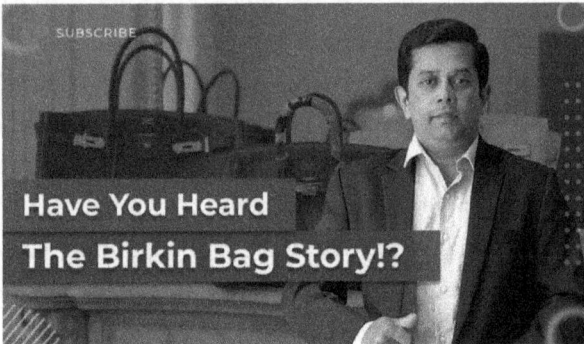

Have You Heard The Birkin Bag Story!?

Visit: https://stardompublishing.com/evenmoreinfo/
-or-
Scan this to play the video

19

WHAT IS THE DIFFERENCE BETWEEN FICTION, NON-FICTION, AND OTHER BOOKS?

BIG IDEA: It is like choosing the right vehicle to reach your destination.

If you have decided to write a book, it is essential that you understand the different genres of books. It is crucial that you have a topic in mind, and are clear on who your target audience is, and what message your book is going to present to the readers. There are many genres of books: fiction and nonfiction are the two major categories. Literature that is created via the imagination is referred to as fiction. All your short stories like The Panchatantra Tales, Vikas Stories for Children, Vikram-Betal tales, Champak stories, and other fairy tales are all considered fiction. While some fiction might be based on real events and true characters, the stories are fabricated, exaggerated, and customized according to the target audiences' needs.

For instance, if you read Stephen King's books, you will notice that many of his stories and novels are set in the fictional town of Derry. Although Derry is not a real place, it is said that the town resembles King's hometown of Bangor. There are many such examples. The fiction genres include mystery, romance, horror, crime, social issues, sci-fi, fantasy, etc. Some of the classic examples of fiction are *To Kill a Mockingbird* by Harper Lee, *Pride and Prejudice* by Jane Austen, *A Tale of Two Cities* by Charles Dickens, *1984* by George Orwell, and many others. Non-fiction, on the other hand, refers to literature that is based wholly and solely on facts. It is the broadest category of literature.

This may include books on business, health and fitness, home and décor, literature, religion, politics, biography, history, self-help, science, etc. Examples include *A brief history of Time* by Stephen Hawking, *Hiroshima* by John Hersey, *The Diary of a Young Girl* by Anne Frank, *This is Water* by David Foster Wallace, and millions of others. Most business books are classified as non-fiction. It is factual, and is based on true reports. Non-fiction is mostly evidence-based books.

There is a fine line between fiction and non-fiction, and as an author, it is important that you understand this difference. Many non-fiction writers end up using flowery language and exaggerated facts to impress the readers. *Cold Blood*, one of the best works of non-fiction, had significantly blurred the line between fiction and non-fiction as Capote's descriptions were so detailed and full of life. In fact, this ended up in many readers questioning the veracity of his account. To add on, back in 2006, James Frey, author of *A Million Little Pieces*, was kicked out of Oprah's Book Club for fabricating most of his memoir. Therefore, if you are a non-fiction writer, you must make sure that your book has references and that everything is factually right. Fiction is elaborate. Here, the author can go on and on without any limits. Plus, different readers interpret fiction in different ways. However, in non-fiction, there is a set word limit and the author must stick to facts. References have to be provided for all the statements.

Nothing, not a thing, can be fabricated. Apart from fiction and non-fiction, other significant categories of books include academic textbooks, biographies, encyclopedias, travel journals, etc.

Now, why do we even need genres? Why can't we just write what we like? Why must we have to stick to set rules while writing a book? Well, I have one simple answer for you: To make the process of reading easier. Let us say you walk into a library in search of a book. Let us assume you are looking for a book on 'How to lose weight in three months.' This is a non-fiction book. Now, imagine you did not have categories in this library. Then you would have to go to every book stand in the library and look for the book. On the other hand, if fiction and non-fiction were already categorized, you would just go to the non-fiction section and pick up your book. Let us now understand a few sub-genres of fiction and non-fiction books:

Sub-Genres of Fiction Books:

- The Classics – *The Great Gatsby, 1984,* etc.
- Historical Fiction – *All the Light We Cannot See, War and Peace, A Tale of Two Cities,* etc.
- Adventure – *Don Quixote, The Three Musketeers, Treasure Island,* etc.
- Western – Think old school cowboy movies, *Doc,* etc.

- Science Fiction – *The Lord of The Rings, The Hitchhiker's Guide to The Galaxy, Ender's Game,* etc.

Genres of Non-fiction Books

- **History:** Books that look at past events. Historical non-fiction can be written as a narrative or as an educational text.
- **Biography or Autobiography:** A biography or autobiography is the story of a particular person's life.

  ➢ **Some of The Different Types of Life Stories are Given Below:**
  - **Autobiography:** When the author discusses their life story.
  - **Memoir:** Like an autobiography, but only about a particular theme or time from the author's life.
  - **Biography:** A life story when the author researches or interviews a subject to tell their life story

- **Philosophy:** An academic view of knowledge and existence. Many philosophy books are incredibly old, with some dating back to ancient times.
- **Health and Wellness:** These books talk about all the possible ways you can get or stay healthy. Some of these books highlight specific medical issues or advise on nutrition, alternative medicine, sex, meditation, and mental wellness.

- **Science:** Science books talk about physical sciences like mathematics, technology, chemistry, biology, physics, engineering, and more.
- **Social Science:** Social science books look at social relationships and relationships. This includes anthropology, sociology, political science, and law books.
- **Psychology:** Books that examine mental and emotional functions and well-being.
- **Self-help:** Self-help books provide techniques and tactics for the readers to pursue self-improvement. These self-help books can be on topics like leadership, motivation, habit creation, productivity, mindset, and more.
- Encyclopedias, book abstracts, business, entrepreneurship, leadership, personal finance and other career-specific books. Books about the house, the garden, agriculture, environment and sustainability.
- **Pet Care:** Books about looking after pets and other animals.
- **Cook Books**: Recipes and the history of food. These cook books can also be in a narrative form, where the author gives context to the importance of the recipe.

Now That You Have Understood the Different Book Genres, I Want You to Ponder on The Following Points:

Do you have a genre you like? If yes, great. If not, read up and pick one. Start exploring now.

RESOURCE: VIDEO

Visit: https://stardompublishing.com/evenmoreinfo/
-or-
Scan this to play the video

20

WHAT IS A 'BESTSELLING' BOOK AND HOW TO WRITE ONE?

BIG IDEA: A bestseller is a book or other media noted for its top selling status, with bestseller lists published by newspapers, magazines, and book store chains.

The 'bestselling' label is something that every author wishes to acquire. Imagine being addressed as a "Bestselling author'. This is indeed every author's dream. It is a mark of distinction. There are many bestseller lists in the world today. These lists are published by some of the prestigious organizations like the Wall Street Journal and the New York Times as well as by online portals like Amazon. These lists are compiled after the sales data of books are collated at the end of every week. These lists are published under the various genres available, both in fiction and non-fiction. The sales data are collected from retailers using the ISBN, and then the lists are generated by the respective publications.

If a book makes it into a bestseller list, it means the book has sold many copies and its reach is widespread. And this could indicate that more people want to buy those books.

Some popular books tend to stay in the bestseller lists for weeks and, in some cases, even months.

If you wish to write and publish a bestseller, you would need to select a popular topic. The publisher will carry out an extensive and concentrated promotion and marketing campaign to make the public aware of your book. When authors choose to work with us, we ensure and prepare the book (and the author) to hit the bestseller list right from the planning stage.

What Makes a Book 'Bestselling'?

Firstly, a great topic. Second, great writing. Third, hard work. That is it. If you have these three in place, your book can undoubtedly become a bestseller. However, it is not going to happen overnight. This chapter will help you understand the process of writing a bestselling book.

Make sure to spend some time on your book every day. Brainstorm ideas and think about all the ways you can make your book creative. Create those pockets of time no matter how busy you are. The first thing you must do when you start your book is create an outline. I know I have said this multiple times. Creating an outline is crucial for your book. Your book should cater to the target audience. Give yourself a deadline and try to stick to it.

Sit in a quiet space when you are working on your book. Read it again and again. You need all your concentration. Write your book and then read it from a reader's perspective. Think about the changes and amendments that can be made. If you have signed up with a publisher, listen to what the editors have to say.

Take in all the inputs because you need all the help you can get. Since you are writing a book on your area of expertise, you cannot afford to make any mistakes. Gather all the references. Pick a style and stick to it. The first-person narrative is usually suggested as it helps you connect with the readers.

As I have already mentioned, make sure you have your outline ready before you start writing your book. A well-developed outline will always be your savior. If it is a self-help book, make sure you write an introduction where you explain to the readers why you are writing a book and what message you want the readers to take home.

How well will the readers be equipped to face life after reading your book? What major questions will your book be answering? Address all these questions in your introduction. Unlike fiction, where you use your imagination and come up with stories to impress the readers, you will have to stick to facts in non-fiction. So, try to come up with a way to make your book creative.

Researching, writing, and editing take a lot of time. Whether you write a little each day or you set aside a couple of days each week to focus solely on your book, create a schedule and a timeline. But stay flexible. The best ideas may come to you when you are standing in line at the grocery store or when you are in the shower. Keep a pen and paper handy, so that you can write down the ideas whenever inspiration strikes. Today, you can also use your mobile phone for this. Use proofreading tools to check your work. This is very, very important. Non-fiction is all about facts, and you cannot go wrong here. Another important thing to do is investing in a good design.

The cover is the face of your book. So, spend a good amount of time designing it. Make sure it holds up what your book is standing for. Once you are done with the content, look for suitable images that can go inside your book. These can be a visual representation of the content or an addition to the text.

Quick Assignment:

Go to Amazon and explore their bestseller lists for different categories.

RESOURCE: VIDEO

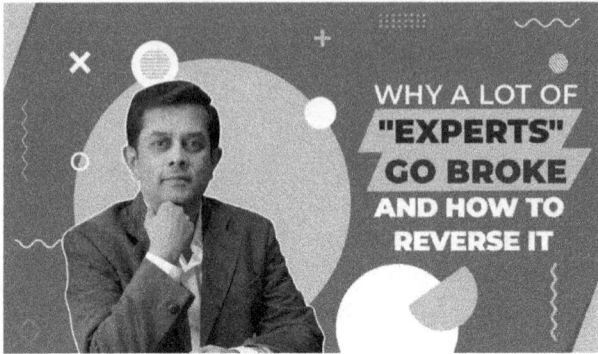

WHY A LOT OF "EXPERTS" GO BROKE AND HOW TO REVERSE IT

Visit: https://stardompublishing.com/evenmoreinfo/
-or-
Scan this to play the video

21

I AM A COACH/TRAINER. HOW CAN I USE A BOOK TO BUILD MY BUSINESS?

BIG IDEA: Your own book could help you position your expertise and attract the right students for your coaching or training sessions.

If you are a coach or a trainer, you can significantly benefit from publishing your own book. Unlike in other fields, trainers need to tell their life experiences or produce some certification to prove their credibility.

Producing a certificate would have been enough in the olden days; however, today, that is not enough. There are many online courses available, and a quick search on the Internet will help you locate more than 20 certified trainers in your very locality. So, while certification is good to have, it will not help you enrol new clients.

How do the best coaches and trainers distinguish themselves from the rest, then? Simple: they write a book. They use a book in the place of a business card or a certificate to attract the right coaching and training prospects for their programs. A published book can position the coach/trainer as an authority on the topic and attract those interested.

Marketing is greatly augmented with a book, and in many cases, it is the only marketing activity needed to get a steady flow of clients. Let us say you run a 'Spoken English' class. Many people seek to learn English in recent times. And given the job competition, 'Spoken English' classes are found on every street today. The competition is fierce. What can you do to stand out from the crowd?

Well, you must understand here that although anyone can claim to be an English tutor, only the credible ones last longer. Let us say you have written a book on 'Spoken English' classes, introducing yourself, your background, the different methods of teaching you employ, and the various benefits of taking your classes.

Additionally, you have a website where you promote your book. This puts you on the map and even people who do not live in your locality will come looking for you. You have established your credibility and gained people's trust. Here is another major advantage of writing a book.

Let us say your sessions cost about $35 an hour. Not everyone can afford to pay $35 an hour, four days every week. So, your book will help those people who cannot attend your sessions. Your book contains the gist of all your sessions, and this information can prove vital to many. Plus, since they have it in the form of a book, they can read it repeatedly.

Here Are Some Other Benefits:

1. You get recognized as the expert. Your book reflects who you are. Your book reflects the knowledge you have about that particular subject. It acts as a certificate of your abilities. Without you saying anything, your readers will know what to expect and how you will be of help to them. Thus, your book also becomes your business card.

2. You get all the media attention. Once you get recognized as an expert, various newspapers and TV channels will reach out to you and ask for your opinions. Your book will be used to address you. This is the best marketing tool ever!

3. You will reach a wider audience. Although motivational speakers and trainers conduct group sessions, life coaches mostly conduct one-on-one sessions. So, for a coach to reach a wider audience, he/she will need more than just word-of-mouth.

   But, let us say you give a free copy of your book to each one of your clients and ask them to pass it on to people who might benefit from the book. Now, that is something. Your book will get passed on to numerous people, and this will fetch you popularity.

Are You a Coach/Trainer/Motivational Speaker Looking To Write a Book? Here Are Some More Tips:

1. Your book defines who you are. So, make sure you talk about yourself and explain how your book will help the readers. Explain the different life approaches you have discussed in the book and back them with references. You will be considered credible only if your sources are

credible. Be clear on who your target audience is. Pick a group and cater to their needs.

2. Explain how your book is different from other self-help books out there.

3. Give links to your videos and blogs in your book. Many coaches are good at oral communication. You can use your book as a tool to enhance your videos and blogs.

RESOURCE: VIDEO

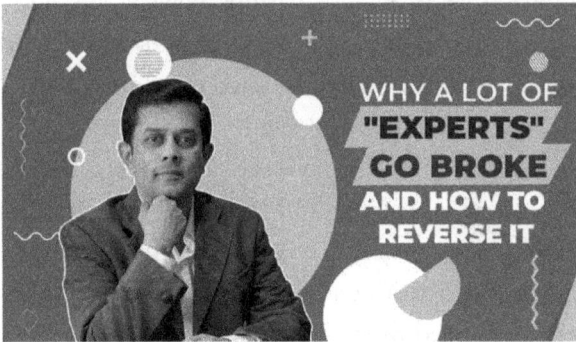

Visit: https://stardompublishing.com/evenmoreinfo/
-or-
Scan this to play the video

22

I AM AN ENTREPRENEUR. I RUN A START-UP. HOW CAN A BOOK HELP ME SUCCEED?

BIG IDEA: Creating value distinction as early as possible can boost success rates for Entrepreneurs.

Writing a book may not be the first thing that comes to your mind when you are trying to find ways to grow your revenue, but it is an option that is well worth exploring in today's digital world. With the right content and a little bit of marketing panache, writing a book relevant to your company's target audience can go a long way in fuelling your company's growth. Watching for some key indicators will help you know if writing a book is a smart idea for your business. (*"Entrepreneur Magazine"*). James Altucher, the author of the bestselling book *Choose Yourself*, once said, "Every entrepreneur should write a book because having a book is the new business card."

If you want to stand out, you need to show your expertise.

Publishing a book is not just putting your thoughts on a blog post. It is an event. It shows your best-curated thoughts, and it shows customers, clients, investors, friends and lovers what the most important things on your mind are right now." If you are an entrepreneur, a book is the very best multipurpose marketing tool you can have.

Start-ups need funding. A book is an excellent investment to seek financing because it will instantly make the author an authority on the topic. Investors want to invest their money with 'experts' and not rookies. Start-ups and entrepreneurs should create a book to build their brand and attract the right support for their ideas.

Again, a book increases your credibility and being credible is important if you are a growing business. It is also a PR opportunity. Let us say your start-up has come up with a fascinating new invention. As the CEO of your company, you have written about your journey of invention. The book gives a detailed look into who you are. It describes your invention and explains how it is going to help people. How exactly is it a PR opportunity?

Well, tech news platforms and magazines are always on the lookout for new content. Once your book hits the market, your PR agent can pitch your book to these platforms. Since it is an innovative invention, along with a book on the same, you will be written about on these platforms. Having written about on news platforms increases your popularity and adds to your credibility. Every coverage that you get is valuable. Thanks to this, your book will become an interview resource for all your future stories, furthering your popularity. You will be invited to talk shows and podcasts.

As I mentioned earlier, many entrepreneurs write books not to get established as an author but to promote their products and services. If you have been in the business for a long time, you would know how important mailing lists are. The larger your list, the greater your potential revenue. You could add to this list by giving away free copies of your book to everyone who subscribes. This way, your books will reach more people, and you will also get more subscribers.

A book increases your visibility and demand. When you write a book, your visibility and credibility in the industry increases. With this comes a natural increase in the number of people who are interested in doing business with you.

Author and entrepreneur Tim Ferriss is a great example of this. Ferriss first achieved worldwide fame with his 2007 book *The 4-Hour Workweek*, based on his earlier entrepreneurial experiences. The book became a New York Times bestseller, earning Ferriss significant coverage in national publications.

As Business Insider reported, Ferriss was able to use his fame to become an angel investor and launch a successful podcast, which has achieved hundreds of millions of downloads. Through a book, Ferriss became one of the biggest names in the industry today. Not every business author will become a New York Times bestseller. But with more demand, you can greatly increase your profitability as you find more lucrative clients (*"Entrepreneur Magazine"*).

Though writing and editing a book require a fair amount of time and research, it can have transformative results for your business. As you use your book to bolster your credibility and expand your market reach, you will be able to grow at a much faster rate than ever before. By writing a book, entrepreneurs can build their personal brand, establish their expertise, and build trust with potential clients

Who Should Write a Book? Should All Entrepreneurs Write a Book?

1. You have just started your company, and you need to spread the word and get more people on board.
2. You have been in the business for some time now and you want to impart knowledge to others on the same path.
3. You want to recruit passionate people. Interestingly, job seekers can also write a book on the job they are passionate about. This will help recruiters.
4. You want to boost sales and get more clients on board.
5. You are an entrepreneur focused on a particular product. However, you are also passionate about something else. So, you write a book and quench your thirst for pursuing other things.
6. You must write a book if you are clueless. Now do not get confused. Let me explain this to you. Writing a book if you have no idea what to do in life is helpful because you are thinking out loud and sharing your thoughts by writing a book. This process will help you clear your mind; your story and thoughts can help someone else who is in the same boat. Plus, having a published book under your name adds to your resume. David Meerman Scott, the American online marketing strategist and author of several marketing books, began writing because he was clueless about life! Now, this man has several books under his belt, including *The New Rules of Marketing and PR.*
7. If you want to network at higher levels of engagement.

8. If you want to get on podcasts and TV shows, or get featured in Newspapers and Magazines.

9. One book will lead to another, and before you know it, you will have three to four books under your name. You would have become a successful writer along with being a successful entrepreneur.

10. You want to become the go-to person.

"The more that you read, the more things you will know. The more that you learn, the more places you'll go."
- Dr. Seuss

23

I AM A DOCTOR. HOW WILL WRITING A BOOK HELP ME?

BIG IDEA: Doctors and Consultants often trade their time for fees. Having a book provides the leverage to not only increase their income but also use their time efficiently.

If you are a Doctor, Professional, or a Consultant, a book can help you attract more high-paying clients as well as establish yourself as the 'sought-after' expert in your field. Here is a personal story. It was the year 2011, and I was sitting at a conference in Los Angeles. Another participant came and sat next to me, and we started networking. It turned out that my co-participant, Andrew Caster, was a medical doctor who specialized in LASIK surgery.

I was wearing glasses, and this had been a needed accessory for me since childhood. Before the seminar's conclusion, Dr Andrew gave me a book he had written about LASIK surgery.

When I returned to my hotel room that day, I opened the book out of curiosity.

The book laid out all there was to know about the procedure and answered the many questions and doubts I had about it. Dr Caster was already a hero in my eyes! The book was interesting and informative, and more importantly, it gave me the confidence to go to Dr. Andrew's clinic the following day for an evaluation. The evaluation turned out to be excellent, and I was qualified for the procedure. A week and $6000 later, I was able to throw away my bulky glasses for good, permanently. The surgery was successful, and even today, after so many years, I am extremely happy with the result.

I knew about LASIK even before I met Dr Andrew, but I did not dare to get under the knife to rectify my vision. I had my own fears, misconceptions, and ideas about the procedure. It was only after I read the book that I was able to visit a LASIK center. That same year, Dr Andrew Caster became one of the country's top two surgeons. He was able to fill his appointment book to the brim with clients ready to pay the premium fee he charged. Do you see the power of using a book as a marketing strategy for a consultant or a professional here?

It is powerful and effective. It pulls paying clients to your practice or program, and you do not have to hawk anything. The book does most of the selling for you. When your prospective clients visit or call you, they are already sold on the idea, for your book has convinced them. All that is left for you to do is tell them the price and show them where to sign.

A book is thus a great marketing tool. It fetches new clients in ways unimaginable. If you give your book to your contacts, they will spread the word. A good review from a happy client will increase your sales. You can send it to people you would like to network with. So, a book will open numerous doors for you. A book will add legitimacy to your expertise. It builds your reputation. How does it do that? Well, let us say you have to visit a consultant, but you are not aware of any names. So, you look up on the Internet. You come up with many names, so you dig a little deeper. You find a so-and-so person with a published book under his or her name.

Who would you choose? A published author or an unknown person? As I mentioned earlier, a book becomes your business card and demonstrates your skills as a consultant. The fact that you have a published bestseller in your name will put you on the map, right at the top, in big bold letters. If you have a book, you need no introduction. Once you gain some popularity, thanks to your book, you will be seen as a thought leader. Your book can increase your name recognition. You will be viewed as a thought leader, and people will recognize your book and your name on the book. It raises your profile as well as respect for your company. This can help when submitting proposals to speak at conferences or to keynote for corporate or association events.

Your book generates attention, raises your visibility, and gives you multiple opportunities for media coverage. A book can position you as the top expert in your field. Now, most people make this mistake. Do not assume that you will get rich from your book sales. Although you might sometimes end up making money through your book sales, most of the time, books are only used as a marketing tool. Most non-fiction books are actually excellent marketing tools. A book certifies your consulting practice and saves you from other tiring marketing practices. A book will make the clients come to you. In fact, this is one of the reasons having a good book title is crucial. Your book title should define your book.

Here Are Some Key Reasons Why a Doctor, Consultant, or a Professional Should Write a Book:

This is true for all areas. You stand out from others when you have a published book in your name. People will come looking for you, thanks to your book. Usually, when people hire doctors, consultants, or professionals, they trust them to help with whatever issue they are facing. This trust is built only when the person knows that you will definitely be able to help them. And how is this trust gained? Your book, of course! Creating a book also helps you refine your ideas and give them a proper structure.

RESOURCE: VIDEO

Visit: https://stardompublishing.com/evenmoreinfo/
-or-
Scan this to play the video

24

I AM A THOUGHT LEADER. HOW WILL PUBLISHING A BOOK BENEFIT ME?

BIG IDEA: Wikipedia defines 'thought leader' as an individual or firm ascribed the quality of 'thought leadership'. Thought leadership is influencing a narrative by understanding what needs to be done.

"A thought leader can be recognized as an authority in a specific field and whose expertise is sought and often rewarded, that can be an expert, a historical figure, or a 'wise person' with worldly impact." (*"Thought leader - HandWiki"*)

Thought leaders, experts, and specialists can build a highly lucrative expert-empire around their expertise with a book. In this case, a book is used to introduce the 'topic' to interested people.

When people show up, they enter a 'marketing funnel,' starting with consuming the content in the book. Some readers become more interested in the topic and seek a deeper understanding of the subject. They end up buying the coaching, training, or consulting programs offered by the expert. It does not stop there.

Some good students would want more in-depth or more engaging experiences and may end up asking for 'one-on-one' coaching, or you can even start your own 'certification program.' *Rich Dad Poor Dad* began as a book series and later evolved into seminars, talk shows, more books, and training programs by the authors, which are now running as multimillion-dollar empires.

If you are a thought leader, you must write a book. When I say the word thought leader, what comes to your mind? Why do you approach thought leaders? Why is thought leadership a must-have aspect in leaders?

Forbes describes the term thought leader as "an individual or firm that prospects, clients, referral sources, intermediaries, and even competitors recognize as one of the foremost authorities in selected areas of specialization, resulting in its being the go-to individual or organization for said expertise." A thought leader drives change and steers trends. The keyword here is 'authority' and authority comes from being an author, right?

The term 'thought leader' or the concept has been around for ages. However, since the dawn of the Internet, the word has found a new meaning. The thought leaders today are entrepreneurs, motivational speakers, or influencers. You are called a thought leader if you are wise and have quick decision-making skills. You are the go-to person and have the authority to address various concerns. So, a book written by a thought leader is highly valued. Given the current times when so many unfortunate things are happening around us, all people need is a little bit of positivity. Thought leaders provide that. Thought leaders bring hope and help to their followers in a big way.

How do you differentiate yourself from others? It is simple: by writing a book. To be a thought leader, you need a combination of experience and innovation.

You must share information, essentially letting people know you are pioneering and that you are knowledgeable through your work. And how do you do that? Again, by writing a book. Thought leaders are not just a source of information and knowledge about a particular field or industry. What sets them apart is that they also use that knowledge to inspire others and help solve their problems, and in the process, create a blueprint for success that any person or organization can replicate in that field.

Let me give you a few examples of some thought leaders across the world who have published books. Kaihan Krippendorff, Founder and CEO at Outthinker Strategy Network, has written four books on business strategy, growth, and transformation. Thomas Koulopoulos, Chairman/Founder at Delphi Group, has written books like *The Gen Z Effect, Cloud Surfing, The Innovation Zone, Smartsourcing: Driving Innovation and Growth through Outsourcing,* and *Corporate Instinct.*

Ton Dobbe, Chief Inspiration Officer at Value Inspiration, has written a book called *The Remarkable Effect: The Essential Book for Tech-Entrepreneurs-on-a-Mission.* Seth W. Godin, an American author and former dot com business executive and the godfather of modern-day marketing, has also written many bestsellers: *The Practice, This is Marketing,* and *What To Do When It's Your Turn.* Anand Mahindra, the Chairman of one of India's most successful global enterprises, is the author of *Change The Rules.* He has also written the book *Reimagining India.*

And you just cannot miss Jon Gordon. He is a consultant, a keynote speaker, and an international author. He has penned several inspirational books like *The Energy Bus, The Coffee Bean,* and *The No Complaining Rule* to name a few.

These are some of the greatest experts in their respective fields, and the books they have written have added value. The world knows they are great because of the books they have authored. You can author a book and become well known too.

Here Are a Few Ways Thought Leaders Could Benefit By Writing a Book:

1. A book gives you credibility. Having the word 'author' in front of your name makes people notice you. You stand out from the crowd.

2. If you are a young thought leader just venturing into the area, a book will make you visible and get you clients. It will get you invited to talks, interviews, and other shows. If you are an established thought leader, then a book will add to your achievements. Plus, you will also be helping and guiding youngsters.

3. If you publish your book internationally, you are noticed by a whole bunch of people. Anybody anywhere can read your book. If people like you, they can connect with you directly through the links to your websites, videos, and blogs and start engaging with you at more deeper levels.

Here Are Some Tips:

1. Again, it is important to understand your target audience:
    If you are a new thought leader, address the common issues faced and resolve them. Give them tips on how to make it to the shore. However, if you are already established, write a book on your own journey and your experiences. Write about how you fought these hurdles and how you made it into the industry. Your book can be more of a self-help book.

2. This is not fiction. Hence, your book does not need to have a positive conclusion. It is okay to talk about real-life issues that people face. You are just stating the facts. But make sure you give your readers hope

and help them achieve their goals. Motivate and inspire them.

3. Write about what youngsters really want to know. You can dedicate an entire chapter to questions and answers. Address all the questions you are generally asked and answer them. This will definitely help others on the same path.

4. I would advise you to stick to a first-person narrative. This will help you connect with the readers. Talking about your life will reassure the readers.

RESOURCE: VIDEO

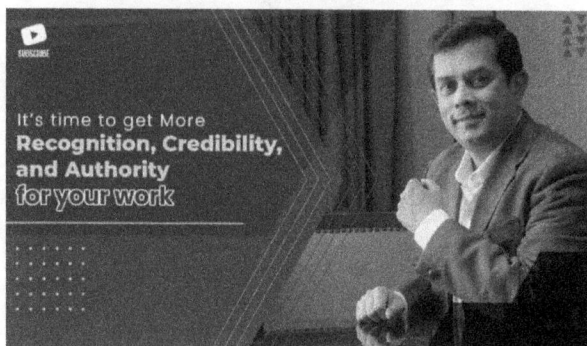

Visit: https://stardompublishing.com/evenmoreinfo/
-or-
Scan this to play the video

A capacity, and taste, for reading, gives access to whatever has already been discovered by others.

- Abraham Lincoln

25

I AM (OR WANT TO BECOME) A PROFESSIONAL SPEAKER. HOW CAN A BOOK HELP ME?

BIG IDEA: The publishing and speaking industries are integrated. Most authors are speakers and most speakers have published books. They complement each other.

One of the primary benefits of having your book is that it can help attract paid speaking engagements. If you were to become a paid speaker, you would also be adding a stream of revenue to your business. You may not believe it, but professional speakers are paid very handsomely, and in fact, it is one of the highest-paying professions. If you are just starting out as a professional speaker, you will be paid anywhere between $2,000 and $5,000 per keynote speech. When you garner experience and build a well-received platform, you would be able to make as much as $20,000, $50,000, or even $100,000 per speaking engagement—take Magic Johnson, Jack Canfield, and Mel Robbins, for instance. If you were to look within

India, speakers like Chetan Bhagat would command fees up to Rs 10 lakh per keynote speaking assignment, plus expenses. However, the benefit of paid speaking is not just the money.

When you speak at large events, you reach out to a wider audience and attract more clients to your core business. Despite the fees charged, event planners still like to schedule speakers who are also authors for a couple of reasons.

The first reason is that the book is an objective piece of evidence that speaks for the author's expertise. It boosts the credibility and reliability of the author. Secondly, the event planners hope to piggyback on the hype and momentum of the author and his/her book. They hope to sell more tickets.

After all, the top priority for any event planner is to make their event a success, and this is usually measured by the number of attendees. This is why whenever event planners want to hire a speaker for an event, they look for people who have written a book on the topic, as it makes their job easier. They can rest easy knowing that the author will not be stumped at any point during the event. They trust the author to be able to tackle the issue at hand.

So, if you have written a book, you are not just establishing your credibility as an expert; you are also putting the minds of event planners at ease. Additionally, because event planners like to make their jobs easier (and who doesn't?), they are likely to choose a speaker who has a book because it allows them to sell something at the back of the room during the event. This is an added incentive for the participants. The more value these event planners give their attendees, the better they look. Back of the room sales are a part of many speaking engagements, and they can boost your sales and business. When you get the audience engaged in your topic, you can also provide greater value addition at the back of the room by doing a book signing.

Once the audience have heard your message and been impressed with your expertise, they are more likely to purchase a book that the author personally autographs for them.

Send Your Book to Event Planners:

This will help you increase traffic, leads, and sales in your business. You can use your book to get established in the speaking domain. Use it as a marketing tool. This is one way you can build your core business. At conferences and events, when you speak for free, you get to sell your product at the premises. You can also build your database by getting business cards from people interested in learning more about your topic.

If you get approval to sell from the stage, you should consider selling a higher-ticket item. Even though you give your book away for free, make sure it is an added value that you provide on top of the higher-ticket item. Now you might ask, what is a higher-ticket item? A higher-ticket item could be an information product, a group-coaching program, or a live event. Whenever it is possible to sell from the stage, take advantage of the opportunity. But first, realize the potential. While your book might bring in $20 per sale, its greatest benefit is to provide you with speaking engagements.

These engagements can attract an audience to whom you can sell something of even greater value, like a $500 coaching package, a $100 product, or a $1,000 private, one-day individualized and tailored coaching session with you. That is an up-sell that boosts your business as well as income. Therefore, whenever an event planner wants you to speak at an upcoming event, you can negotiate a package deal that includes you and your book. For instance, if the seating capacity at the venue is 500, the planners could make a bulk purchase of your book to distribute to the entire audience, or they could purchase a set number of copies for their organization.

Types of Speaking Engagements

Now that you know how your book can help you get speaking engagements and boost your business and income, let us look at the different types of speaking engagements available. There are three basic types of speaking engagements:

1. Speaking for free
2. Keynote speaking
3. Speaking on a stage

Speaking for free is an opportunity for you to put yourself in the spotlight. It is usually a joint venture with a person or an organization who already has established a community that will attend their events. You gain exposure, speaking experience, and a ready-made audience who can become future leads, clients, customers, and book buyers. When you speak for free, you want to make sure you are providing something of value. Make sure to carry some copies of your book to these events.

The best-case scenario will have you walk in, armed with your book and an offer that you can pitch. The product you offer should be valuable to both you and your audience. You may complain about giving free speeches, but you could easily recoup that money when you sell your book and a $500 group coaching package or seminar at the same event. Now, do you see how offering your speeches for free can be beneficial? The second type of speaking is the keynote address.

Keynote speakers are some of the highest-paid speakers in the industry. Those who book keynote speakers usually do not want them making a sales pitch from the stage. They prefer that the speaker spends the entire time on the stage sharing with the audience his/her expertise and insights. Keynote speaking can offer the option to sell your books from the back of the room. You could also opt for a more creative step, like giving each member of the audience a free book in exchange for their business cards. Now, what value does a business card hold?

It contains the contact information of a person. It will provide you with details like the name of the person, job title, telephone number, website, and e-mail address. You could use this information and build up a database of future potential clients. You could up-sell them in the future and continue to provide them with something of value.

Speaking from the stage is the third type of speaking engagement. This can be a free event, as well. However, these events are of a different scale as they can command a large audience of 500 or more people. You would be speaking at large trade shows, association events, or at huge conferences. For instance, corporate events or summits in Las Vegas usually incorporate speaking from the stage. When speakers participate in such events, they are not enticed by the remuneration; rather, it is the audience that attracts them. At an event of this caliber, it is not uncommon to pitch products that are valued at $1,000 or more.

Securing Speaking Engagements

You have got a book, and now you are ready to step on the stage and start your speaking career. But how are you going to attract such engagements? You can send event planners two things: your book and your bio. What most speakers tend to neglect in their attempts to secure speaking engagements is their bio. A bio is more than a laundry list of what you have done—it is your sales pitch!

So, to attract event planners, your bio has to sell you such that you look better than the competition. It has to pack your experience, but it also has to have that oomph that tells them just why you and only you are the perfect speaker for their event! How do you write a bio that will capture attention? How do you stand out?

Here Are Some Things That Your Speaker Bio Should Contain If You Want to Give Yourself an Edge in What Is a Highly Competitive and Crowded Field:

1. Open your bio with your most impressive accomplishment. Did you appear on Oprah? Did you write a bestselling book? Are you the most prominent in your industry? Have you been featured in 47 magazines and periodicals?

2. Did you invent a product or a philosophy? What do you know that nobody else knows? Whatever it is that will grab their attention, use it here in the opening; do not let it get lost down the page. Modesty is not a virtue that will help you stand out; instead, it will put you back into the pack!

3. Follow your most impressive accomplishments with proof that you are an expert. How many years have you worked in the industry? Do you own a business? Have you received awards and recognition from esteemed organizations/agencies? Hey, did you write a book?

These details automatically establish you as an expert in your field, so be sure to talk about it here.

4. The next part of your bio should reveal what unique knowledge or insight you will impart to the audience. When you are done speaking, what will the audience take away? Will they be so inspired and motivated that they just would not be able to sit still? Will they gain a proven success strategy? Will they learn of the ten steps to achieve millionaire status? Whatever it is, make sure you include it in this third section of your bio. You can find the information to include in this section by asking yourself, "What will I bring to the audience that nobody else can?" Finish your bio by giving them something personal they can relate to.

   You want the people reviewing your bio to connect with you and be impressed with what you know. Have you visited all 50 states in the USA? Can you speak eight different languages?

5. Did you personally meet Joe Biden or Kamala Harris or have your picture taken with the Governor or an Oscar-winning actor? Are you connected with the Napoleon Hill Foundation, or did you have the pleasure of meeting a celebrity?

6. Maybe you are the go-to person for the president of an MNC and have a picture you can include from when you received the Employee of the Year Award from a Fortune 500 company.

7. Make your bio professional by keeping it as brief and to the point as possible. But you could jazz it up with some of your unique personality and give the reader a flavor of your style. Include a high-resolution photograph and

a brief summary of the topics you are available to speak on.

If your bio includes these things, and specifically in this order, opening and closing with impressive details, it will definitely get you those lucrative speaking engagements and help you build your portfolio. Once prepared, your bio becomes a promotional tool that stands out from the crowd. Your book makes it even more unique. Because you are an author, you would be considered the authority (The genesis of the words author and authority can be traced to the Latin word *auctor*, which means master, leader, or author!).

A book validates your standing as an expert in your industry. Do you guide people in their relationships or train them in their fitness endeavors? If there is a book with your name and picture on its cover, it will help in generating interest in you and your message. It grants a certain gravitas to your expertise. It flexes your superiority over someone who has not authored a book. With a book and a speaker's bio, you are ready to polish your skills and gain the experience that will make you a sought-after speaker.

If You Do not Yet Have the Experience, There Are Several Things You Can Do, Rather Easily, To Polish Your Speaking Abilities:

I would highly recommend that you join the organization called Toastmasters International. As the name suggests, this organization promotes communication and speaking skills through its clubs in a number of countries. Only those who are comfortable speaking in front of groups can be considered the best speakers. If you do not have a Toastmasters organization near you, join any other local organization that will refine your speaking skills and instil confidence and a sense of ease and comfort in your craft and skill. They will help you confront your stage fright.

One trait that accomplished speakers have developed is their ability to connect with their audience. You should also look to develop this skill. Practice makes perfect—this should be your mantra when you join organizations like Toastmasters. Practise, gain experience, and also network with others in the speaking industry.

My advice would be to start small. If there are local libraries and rotary clubs near you, find out if they have speaking opportunities for you to volunteer for. Do not ignore the possibilities of being a guest speaker for a writers' association, a parents' group, or an advisory group. Many such organizations and clubs in every community are looking for people to share valuable content with their audience.

Send a letter, along with your speaker's sheet, and let them know that you are available to speak at their next monthly meeting. There are manifold benefits when you speak at such avenues. They not only help you in building your experience, but they will also add to a growing list of accomplishments on your resume.

Another significant benefit is that it will also greatly expand your scope, and it will increase your exposure within the community. Soon, organizations will begin contacting you as the go-to expert in your field.

Once you feel that you have built up enough experience, take to the road. When you have published a book and established yourself as a reputable speaker in the local media and your community, expand your reach.

There will be many seminars and workshops organized by esteemed organizations and individuals in your industry. Attend the relevant ones and look to connect with the hosts and participants of such events. They are prospective clients who would be looking for a speaker in the future.

Promote yourself through professional speaking sites and organizations. Make sure you include the positive feedback and testimonials you have received in the past. With your expertise, experience, promotional material (speaker's bio), and your book, you have everything to offer the next time someone is looking for the perfect speaker for their next event. As you can see, opportunities abound for you to boost your business and make money by selling your book, your product, or your services through speaking engagements. It is one of the greatest ways to use your book, and there is no greater proof that your book is one of the most powerful marketing tools you have available. Use it!

RESOURCE: VIDEO

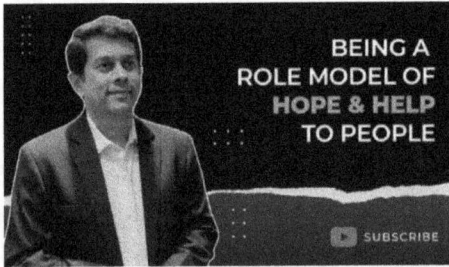

Visit: https://stardompublishing.com/evenmoreinfo/ -or- Scan this to play the video

26

SELF-ASSESSMENT: CAN I REALLY ACCOMPLISH MY GOAL OF BECOMING AN AUTHOR?

Here is a quick self-assessment you can take to determine whether you have all it takes to jump on this journey of becoming an author. This assessment is based on goal-attainment theory. Score yourself on a scale of 1 to 10 for each attribute below:

1. Future Identity - Do you clearly see yourself as a published author in the future?

0 .... 5 10
Me!? An author?   You bet! I want to
It's so weird.   become a bestseller!

2. Internal Value - Is this something I am passionate about, would enjoy doing, and feel proud of?

0 .... 5 10
Nah! It's too scary   Hell Yeah! It's my
or embarrassing.   Big Dream!

3. Utility Value - Does this goal lead to a beneficial outcome for me?

0 .... 5 10
No, I don't think so.   Of course, it's a big yes!

4. Writer Confidence - Am I confident enough as a writer?

0 .... 5 10
Well, I can barely   I will figure it
write an email.   out for sure.

5. Courage Level - Am I willing to put my thoughts out there irrespective of the critics?

0 .... 5 10
Critics and trolls   My thoughts can be useful
scare the shit out of me.   So, I will forge ahead.

6. Reader Value - Will my readers gain confidence and capability from my book?

0 .... 5 10
I don't know.   Of course. Readers
Maybe none.   come first.

7. Resource Allocation – Am I willing to put in the necessary time, energy, and investment to see the project through?

0 .... 5 10
I am impulsive   I always complete
and quit easily   whatever I start.

8. Decision Authority - Am I having the power and authority to make and own my decisions?

0 .... 5 10
No, I have to ask my
spouse, partner, or the tooth fairy!

Yes, I have control and
authority over decisions.

9. Coach-ability - Am I willing to work with a publishing coach and follow the recommendations?

0 .... 5 10
I don't like to get
coached. I hate it.

I'd love to work with
a qualified coach.

10. Growth Orientation – What is my attitude toward growth and progress? (0 – Perfectionist, 10 – Excited with progress)

0 .... 5 10
I am a strict
perfectionist.

I get excited with a
steady progress.

How Did You Do?

If you scored less than 25, - Sorry... writing and publishing your own book is not a good idea right now. Get free access to a 5-part online course at www.stardompublishing.com/first-book.html to learn more.

If you scored between 26 and 50, - You lack clarity and control to decide whether a book is a suitable goal for you. Get a copy of the book "Write Now" at www.WriteNowBook.com and explore this idea.

If you got between 51 and 75, - You are super-ready... speak to a qualified "Publishing Advisor" to learn how to create and publish your own book at:
www.StardomAlliance.com/meeting

Got between 76 and 100? - You should have started your book last year! Go to www.StardomBooks.com right now (or speak to a qualified "Publishing Advisor" at: www.StardomAlliance.com/meeting)

Access videos, downloads, and additional training on how to quickly and easily create your own books by visiting: www.StardomPublishing.com/moreinfo

ANSWERS TO COMMON QUESTIONS

"I do not have time to write a book!... What should I do?"

Nobody has a lot of time today and we work with 'busy' experts like you. That is why at Stardom Books, we have created the 'Rapid Book Creation' system that allows aspiring authors to create their own books in less than 30 hours of their time. In fact, they can even 'speak' their book, if they are not comfortable with writing. We have a SYSTEM to create their bestselling book that they will be proud to present to the world, WITHOUT taking months or years of their time. They are just asked to follow the 9-step plan and they will know they are in good hands.

"How does this make sense?"

On an average, EXPERTS spend over $40,000 (₹3,00,000) a year on networking, seminars, certifications, and conferences. How much do YOU spend? Imagine how you can leverage these opportunities with your OWN book!

According to the Bureau of Economic Analysis, consumers spend their money as follows: Food: 36,129, Housing: 2,93,557, Clothes: 60,700, Transportation: 1,13,677, Healthcare: 45,157, Entertainment: 68,504, Insurance: 23,373, and Everything Else: 1,18,012. All these figures are 'per' person.

A one-time investment for your OWN book is measly when compared to all these recurring expenses, right? The new

Samsung SUHD curved television set costs a whopping ₹4,23,000 ($55K). What gives you more pride, reputation, and authority: a TV set shaped like a curve or a BOOK in your name?

"The investment is too high or I do not have the budget for a book project; what to do?"

It really depends on how to approach this.

If you try to do it on your own, probably you may end up creating a wrong asset (a book is a valuable asset) for your business or profession.

With my coaching, you are guaranteed to create a bestselling book. And this deal is actually better than free. You get 100% royalties to cover the investment and then 50% for life. Is this free or better than free?

It is an opportunity that pays you to create an incredible asset for your business or profession. Plus, you also get free copies of your book.

Let me ask you this: "Do you send your children to a local government school just because it is lower priced?"

"How is Stardom Books different from others?"

First of all, Stardom Books is not just a publisher or a printer. We are a 'Hybrid' publishing house that focuses on helping you become a 'Thought Leader' or an 'Influencer' in your niche. Helping you create and publish your book is just one part of this program, which is integrated with video presence, personal branding, media exposure, expert positioning, and your bigger mission in life. So, it is an integrated and holistic approach that nobody else is offering.

And the best part is...with Stardom, you always own the copyrights and I.P. (intellectual property) of your book. With us, it is a partnership.

Is it not better to pay a little extra and get the best value than try to cut corners by going for cheap services and hurting your image after your book is published? I am sure you do not want to trust your reputation and identity with mediocre players.

"Can you take my investment from the royalties I am going to earn in the future? Or "Can I start this project without an investment?"

We wish we could do that, but it is not possible to start a project WITHOUT your investment, because this goes directly into the production cost. The project needs various resources like editors, writers, designers, proofreaders, and publishing experts, in addition to hard costs like fees, taxes, registrations, printing, stationery, mock-ups, distribution costs, and a number of other direct expenses to create a bestselling book. And, we do not cut corners here because we hire the world's best team, so that our authors can enjoy the best services.

To make it even more reasonable for you, we are providing free author copies as part of the project, so that you get back your investment in the form of books. Apart from this, authors also get to recover their investment first from the royalties. So, essentially, for all the services we provide and the resources we bring to the project, all we are asking our authors to do is to pick up a few hundred copies of their own book. Fair enough?

"Okay, but do you have ANY option that will not need an investment to work with Stardom Books"

Well... Of course, there are rare exceptions.

- If you a serving defence personnel, we will work out a special deal for you, along with thanking you for your services.

- If you are under the age of 12, we have a separate 'Stardom Books Junior' program for young writers.

- Aspiring authors with disabilities are welcome and encouraged to work with Stardom Books at special rates.

- Online influencers and celebrities having 200,000 or more fans and followers (combined on LinkedIn, Facebook, or Instagram) get special book deals (no other forms of followers are eligible).

"What happens if I wait?"

Nothing really... except your investment goes up. Your time left comes down. Our bandwidth will also get filled up frequently and you will have to get on a wait list to start your project with us.

"Can I do it on my own?"

Of course. You can always 'self-publish' your book..., build your own house..., do self-medication..., teach yourself, or become a one-person army and do everything on your own, with your own resources. Or..., you can use leverage.

What we offer at Stardom is an ELITE program where we work with you to design and create a bestselling book with our consulting, tutorials, templates, and training.

Once your book is ready, it will become an Internationally Published Work from a reputed publisher, when you work with us.

We also take care of editing, proofreading, cover designs, formatting, platform integrations, enhancements, and the complete publishing suite for worldwide distribution on various platforms.

On the other hand, if you want to do everything on your own, the project will not only cost you money to bring in all the resources needed but you will also have to factor the cost of your own time away from your business or profession to do this project.

Considering all this, is it not smart to work with us to become an internationally published, bestselling author?

"How do I get an agent or a publisher?"

If you are looking for traditional ways to getting published, you will probably need a literary agent who will connect you with the publishers in your genre.

You will then need to submit your book proposal to multiple publishers and wait for one of them to respond. It is not unusual to get rejected by multiple publishers.

It has happened to numerous, even really famous authors like JK Rowling (Harry Potter), Brendon Burchard, and Dave Asprey, and my first book was rejected by traditional publishers as well (before I started my own publishing company).

The best way to find an agent is by asking other traditionally published authors for referrals. Another way is to participate in literary events.

Finding a publisher to publish your book the traditional way is a numbers game. Be prepared to reach out to dozens of publishers, submit book proposals, wait for months (sometimes years) to get a reply, and finally get rejected or get accepted.

The easier way is to work with a 'Hybrid' publisher like Stardom Books.

"What should I write about?"

This is a common question by first-time authors. In fact, this one quick question has clipped the wings of many experts, entrepreneurs, and professionals from becoming published authors because they could not come up with a satisfying answer to this question. They think, either they do not know as much as required to write a book or everything they know has already been written by someone else!

That is why there are multiple chapters that cover multiple angles to this question in this book.

I am sure you can find the answer and the clarity you are looking for, in one of those chapters.

"How to get book reviews?"

Well, once your book is published, the next important step is to get as many reviews as possible for your book on various platforms.

People will not leave a review unless you specifically ask them. So, do not forget to include a review request within the book. Other sources of reviews are friends, followers, and social contacts. Swap reviews with other authors. You can also find reviewers online.

Search for the specific genre on your favourite book seller's website and reach out to them with a review request in exchange for a free copy of your book. Reviews should be fair, impartial, and non-incentivized.

Newspaper and magazine editors also do book reviews. Reach out to such publications.

Industry associations often have newsletters. A book review can easily go into one of those issues.

Get in touch with the editors and send them your information. At Stardom Books, we provide a 'media kit' for our authors that has worked wonders in getting published reviews.

"Should I just go for an e-book or publish a print edition as well?"

E-books, paperbacks, hardcover editions, and audiobook editions are different types of 'consumption' preferences by people. Even though the content inside is the same, the way the material is read and absorbed (or used) by the end users are different for each medium.

E-books can be delivered instantly whereas the paperback edition allows for making notes and markings. Hardcovers are preferred by readers who value durability and quality whereas audiobooks are preferred by people who listen to content while traveling or exercising. At Stardom Books, all our books are published in both the print and digital formats by default.

"How to judge the success of my book?"

The term 'success' is arbitrary in this context. For some authors, getting their message out is success. For some others, influence matters. For someone else, hitting the bestseller list is the goal, while a few others may see success when they feel their contributions are acknowledged.

This is why at Stardom Books, we start our author programs by doing an exercise to determine the meaning of 'success' for each other before they decide the 'topic' of their books. Based on the author's goals and aspirations, a certain 'type' or 'genre' of book is suggested by our publishing experts.

"Should I write my book alone or bring in a co-author?"

Almost all books (99%) are written solo. If you have a contributing partner, spouse, or a researcher, you can bring them along as a co-author. The *Rich Dad Poor Dad* series of book is a great example. Co-authors can bring in their own perspective or help you in research for the book: *Blue Ocean Strategy* was co-authored by two authors.

A book is an almost permanent entity that can exist for many years after publication. So, choose your co-author wisely, if you prefer to take this route.

"What is the ideal book size?"

For non-fiction categories like business, trade, professional, how-to, self-help, motivation, inspiration, personal legacy, etc., the ideal book length would be around 150–200 pages. It roughly translates to about 30K–50K words. If there are illustrations, pictures, and charts, the number of words could be even lesser.

The physical size of most of the books sold in this category is 8.5 inches tall by 5.5 inches wide and 6 X 9 (trade paperback). Non-fiction books are usually terse and to-the-point, and hence need to be really trim and edited tightly.

Fiction, however, is quite the opposite. The thicker it is, more the entertainment and higher the value. Non-fiction is about sharing knowledge, teachings, or training, or sharing key ideas, and hence, shorter the better. However, books shorter than 120 pages in length do not sell well (according to global book buying statistics). So, keeping the finished book to about 150–200 pages in length would be considered as ideal.

"Should I write a book on my personal journey?"

When figuring out what kind of book to create, most first-time authors have the idea of writing about their 'personal journey' or 'life lessons'. Well… I am not against writing a biography, but that is not the best KIND of book to create for most people.

The best book is the one that aligns with your BIG WHY… It should help you accomplish a goal or be an aspiration. AND, most importantly, the best book solves a problem and becomes USEFUL for the readers. Your personal stories, anecdotes, journey, etc., will become 'part' of your book, while the topic itself is focused on your readers and not on yourself. However, there are exceptions where an extraordinary story or a personal journey can become a bestseller as well.

Discuss with your publishing advisor or coach to figure out the best course of action for your situation.

"Who owns the copyright to the book?"

Technically, the author should own the complete rights to everything in the book. That is how we write our 'author-publisher' contracts at Stardom Books. However, some publishers may try to keep the copyrights to themselves and hold the author at their mercy. So, look out for those clauses in the contract before you sign.

As soon as a book is published (by a publishing house), the content inside the book will automatically become copyrighted by virtue of its publishing. This is good for most people. However, if you want even more protection and the ability to sue others, your work should be separately registered with the specific copyright registration authorities, like the US copyrights authority in the USA.

ACTION GUIDES
for all these amazing books

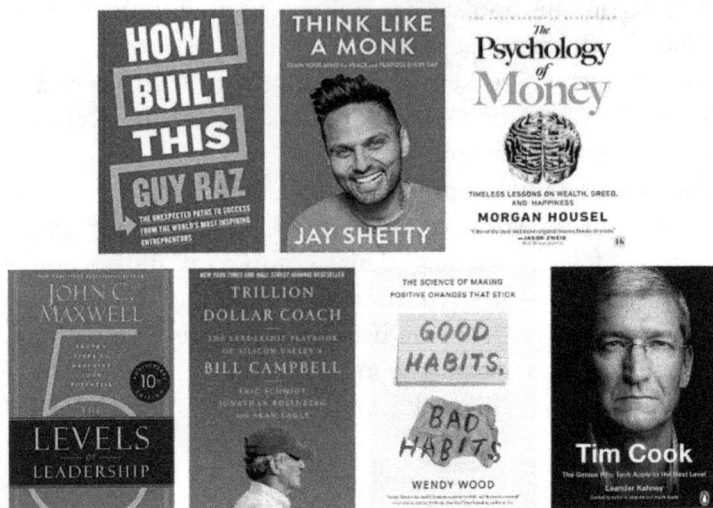

Includes **Book Summary, Reading Plan, Capture Ideas and Action Plan** for each book.

Download the action guides here:
http://RaamAnand.com/action-guides

ABOUT THE AUTHOR

RAAM ANAND

2-times Bestselling Author
Publishing Advisor to Top Leadership
Investor in Various Start-ups
Chief Editor & Publisher
High-performance Coach
Founder of Several Businesses in N. America & India
Supports Various Causes & Movements

Raam Anand coaches non-writers and first-time author aspirants to become published authors. He advices leaders on high-performance and becoming more influential and persuasive. Raam Anand is a two-times international bestselling author and one of the most followed and respected leadership and publishing coaches in the world.

In his role as the Chief Editor at Stardom Books (USA/India), Raam has published more than 200 books and coaches people on high-performance, influence, personal branding, and book publishing.

According to industry statistics and magazine reports, Raam is one of the world's leading coaches in the industry. He built multiple businesses in North America and Asia, grossing several millions of dollars in revenue. He has trained hundreds of thousands of CxO's, Experts, Entrepreneurs, Professionals, and Thought leaders through his books, online courses, video training, and his live workshops, seminars, and conferences.

Raam has spent over 20 years researching, coaching, and training on business and high-performance to bring you the very best strategies for improving your business, life, and well-being.

Focus:

1. Work with the Top Management, CxOs, Business Leaders, Thought Leaders, Experts, Olympic Athletes, Other Coaches, and Trainers to help them achieve higher levels of performance and potential.
2. Help people (non-writers) find and spread their message in a big way and turn their knowledge into a successful book from Stardom Books (USA/India), one of the fastest growing hybrid publishing companies on the planet.
3. Coach and Train Experts, Entrepreneurs, and Professionals at "Experts-Leadership-Academy" on how to "10x" their wealth and business by building their own "expert-empires" around their knowledge and expertise.
4. Organize national and international seminars like "Super Achievers Summit", "10x Wealth & Biz", "Experts Leadership Academy", "Business Conclave" and so on.
5. Launch reputed speakers in India, like Sharon Lechter (co-author of *Rich Dad Poor Dad* series of books) with full liaison and support.

For joining Raam's "Live Limitless" movement, visit RaamAnand.com. For additional information on our companies and brands, please visit StardomAlliance.com

StardomBooks.com | StardomPublishing.com

BOOK RAAM AS A SPEAKER AT YOUR EVENTS

For over a decade, Raam Anand has been educating, entertaining, motivating, and inspiring business owners, entrepreneurs, start-ups, VP and C-level executives, coaches, consultants, advisors, experts, and professionals to build their platforms, amplify their message, and become thought leaders, authorities, and celebrity influencers.

He can guide any audience step-by-step on how to build and grow any business with bestselling books, online marketing, social media, mobile, and product creation strategies that are proven to work.

His origin story includes his transformation over the last two decades, going from an under-privileged, middle-class family kid to becoming the top leader and coach around the world with no backing and no investment. After successfully building multiple businesses and brands across North America and India, Raam can share relevant, actionable strategies that anyone can use—even if they're starting from scratch.

His unique style inspires, empowers, and entertains audiences while giving them the tools and strategies they need and want to get seen and heard to build and grow successful sustainable brands and businesses.

Raam has trained, coached, spoken to, and helped Billionaires, Olympic coaches, Top Executives, Experts, Entrepreneurs, and Professionals in various industries across the globe.

RAAM SPEAKS ON A VARIETY OF TOPICS:

- High-Performance
- Influence and Persuasion
- Rapid Book Publishing
- Personal Branding
- Innovation and Product Creation
- Speaking/Selling from the Stage
- Strategic Marketing
- Selling Like Superstars
- Speechcraft
- Stagecraft
- 6 Critical 'Book-Writing' Questions for Leaders/Doctors/Experts/CxOs
- Book-Writing Best Practices for Leaders/Doctors/Experts/CxOs
- Is Writing a Book the Right Choice for You or Not!?
- How to Write a Business or Professional Book (for Non-Writers)
- Why Should You Write a Book & How To Do It EVEN If You've Never Done It Before
- 9 Secrets of the World's Highest Achievers
- Writing a Book for Your Business or Profession: Best Practices
- Writing a Book While Leading a Team
- Writing a Book While Running a Company
- Doctors: Writing a Book for Your Patients
- Book Writing for Busy [AVATAR] /Leaders/Doctors/Experts/CxOs
- How To Choose Your Book Writing Coach?
- Biography Vs. Memoir Vs. Non-fiction - Choosing the type of Book to Write

HOW TO BOOK RAAM AS A SPEAKER:

Email info@stardomalliance.com or
call +1(302)-504-4257 (USA) or
93804 54426 (India)

WRITE YOUR OWN BOOK!

ARE YOU USING THE #1 STRATEGY FOR INFLUENCE, PR, BRANDING, SALES, MARKETING & CREDIBILITY?

SCHEDULE A FREE, NO-OBLIGATION APPOINTMENT WITH OUR PUBLISHING ADVISORS TO DISCUSS.

Schedule a free appointment with our
Publishing Advisor to discuss your book idea:

http://StardomAlliance.com/meeting

www.ingramcontent.com/pod-product-compliance
Lightning Source LLC
Chambersburg PA
CBHW031512040426
42445CB00009B/189